THE GREATER BODY: STUDIES IN AMERICAN NEOROMANTICISM

THE GREATER BODY: STUDIES IN AMERICAN NEOROMANTICISM

William Young

TABLE OF CONTENTS

AUTHOR'S NOTE

These studies trace the development of a mid and late twentieth century romanticism, a NeoRomanticism distinct from both an earlier High Modernism and a later Postmodernism. The first four essays focus on five mid-century writers, all but one American: D.H. Lawrence (English, and also a precursor), Paul Bowles, Robert Lowell, John Ashbery, and William Stafford. The remaining three essays address more recent writers, all of them American, Raymond Carver, Tim O'Brien, Brian Young, and Jenny Mueller. These latter writers exhibit strong romantic tendencies but variously also exhibit, to a greater degree than the first grouping, counter-romantic, minimalist, and (with Ashbery) postmodernist tendencies. A personal note enters at times into the discussion of this latter set, since I met all of them (on the other hand, only Stafford of the first set).

I wish to acknowledge Roger Bowen for his helpful suggestions and criticisms in response to earlier drafts of this manuscript as well as for his unflagging encouragement of its author. I am also grateful to Darryl Hattenhauer and Tenney Nathanson for their editorial suggestions and criticisms.

Earlier versions of parts of this manuscript appear in the pages of *The Arkansas Review, The Denver Quarterly*, and *The Midwest Quarterly*. I am pleased to thank the various editors for their support.

How to begin to find a shape–to begin again turning the inside out...

William Carlos Williams

...giving a form to inner life *from outside*, from another consciousness.

Mikhail Bakhtin

You shall stand by my side and look in the mirror with me.

Walt Whitman

INTRODUCTION

The writers surveyed in these pages fall more or less outside of, in terms of both chronology and intention, the matrix of Late Symbolism or High Modernism Edmund Wilson, in *Axel's Castle*, points to in his discussion of W.B. Yeats, Paul Valery, T.S. Eliot, Marcel Proust, James Joyce, and Gertrude Stein. The writers here discussed differ from Wilson's representative high moderns in that they pursue, to varying and various degrees, what Wilson himself calls a "life of pure action and more primitive civilizations" (an attitude he associates with Arthur Rimbaud). Such writers are romantics–or more accurately, "neoromantics" as they belong to the second wave or twentieth century version of romanticism. In response to what Edmund Wilson rightly identifies as the key twentieth-century concern, consciousness, neoromantics shift the ground from High Modernism's tradition-consciousness, that is, the "self" forged through the analysis of and remaking of inherited cultural traditions, to an other-consciousness, the "self" exposed and transformed through contact with distant (yet strangely familiar) lands.

Neoromantics tend toward a greater interest in travel and adventure, work in more intimate, voice-centered as opposed to mythic, technique-centered modes, and tend toward plainly personal-social as opposed to symbolical-aesthetic interpretive models. Such texts are a reaction to the submerging of "self" in High Modernism.

These experiential, confessional, and expressionist modes reorient the self-in-culture alignment of High Modernism toward a self/landscape or self/other vision. The lyric structure of epic memory–my definition of High Modernism–which neoromantics inevitably inherit from their precursors, is countered by a desire to find some alternative to the cul-de-sac of self-analysis and aestheticism latent in the inheritance.

Late Symbolism and High Modernism's inclusive and sublimating stream of consciousness–the whole of which is presented in a somewhat detached and ironic manner–tends to submerge Self and Other within interior monologue and unified symbolic sites. The method is primarily a rendering of states of mind through the symphonic interplay of light and color. The central preoccupation is time and memory. One work discussed in this book, Tim O'Brien's *In the Lake of the Woods,* is to a significant extent late symbolist and high modernist (and postmodernist) in precisely such ways as I've mentioned. And, of course, so are the other works discussed, if to a lesser extent. Yet a difference remains, I believe, in the work of those I've chosen to discuss, including O'Brien's. The neoromantic seeks to relandscape the self by venturing outward; venturing outward he both empties and refurbishes the self. He is still highly self-conscious, as all moderns must be, but he has seen new things, new sides of himself. In a sense, he is born again, the key figures in neoromanticism almost to a man raised in (northern) Protestant cultures. Authenticity, a Protestant and also Existentialist virtue mined in Neoromanticism, is found on the road, on backroads, where, so its believed, authentic cultures still exist. The Protestant or Existentialist's credo is reformulated in America in journeys Midwestern and Far Western. The (far) Midwest is especially central–Whitman's prairies or Jack Kerouac's Denver[1]. Indeed neoromantics go in search of some far Middle of the World (in Bowles case, variously south), where they imagine some sort of insouciant natural man still exists.

Yet in the end the Other–however exotic or primitive–turns out to be a kind of mirror of the self, a listener, or in Whitman's terms, a "camerado." Or, in Joseph Conrad's terms, a "secret sharer." Art, especially romantic art, and particularly modern romantic art, is about *telling* secrets, as Conrad was among the first to fully explore. The challenge for the writer is to create a dramatic form in which he can spy on himself, overhear himself. And in which we, as readers, can spy on ourselves. The first requirement is to, in Lawrence's words, experience one's self being "canceled out." Often this takes place as a result of an encounter with a foreign and previously unacknowledged Other. Once canceled out, one begins to see one's self in strangers–Catherine seeing herself in Heathcliff, for example, or Kit, in Paul Bowles's *The Sheltering Sky*, in a passing nomadic tribe of Arab men. Romantics and especially neoromantics are willing to speak their passions more openly, are willing to tell the truth, however shameful or belated or difficult to articulate; they expose themselves for what they are, hurt, hungry, incomplete, without prospects, thus finally *not* separate from the world around them. The challenge is not only a confessional one, but also a hermeneutic and heuristic one: the job is to translate the hints, the hard-to-identify feelings and longings–lost selves–into human, intimate terms and into action. And only by plundering and unhousing the self do we wind up back where we started, fresh, ready for life and death.

Romantics want to recover old emotional ground, associated with childhood. They want to be free in the world, but free consciousness leads them back to childhood, to early music. This is the romantic double-bind. Early music offers the deep pleasure of a social contract–and an intimate one–without a lot of the encumbering weight of institutionalized traditions; yet a return to a quasi-childhood can sabotage mature expressions of civic responsibility and faith. Can romantic freedom support ethical conduct, democratic processes, and spiritual growth? Walt Whitman pursued just such a question. Indeed it is often the romantic type who most fully explores questions such as the relation of individual freedom to social contract since it is the romantic who tends to approach life in terms of dualities and polarities–childhood and adulthood, self and other, male and female, individual and nation.

As Richard Poirier notes, D.H. Lawrence's character Ursula in *Women in Love* makes the case for "freedom together" (qtd. in Poirier 46). The risk of going out of your own or traveling too far from social circles is solipsism, a risk that becomes every more prevalent in post-modernist-tending texts. Among my "neoromantics" only Lawrence and Stafford seem strongly grounded in a substantial local culture, one they've known since childhood. Mueller as well in some respects. (Among high modernists, Joyce and Faulkner–and Yeats, whom I'd label early modernist–hold a similar advantage.) Bowles, Lowell, O'Brien often seem strangely unmoored. Ashbery and Young do also but they have learned to make that their mooring. In contemporary writing we must turn to pastoralist Philip Larkin or outdoorsman/ novelist Jim Harrison, for example, to find a renewed sense of local grandeur. Or differently, Carver. The renewed appreciation for the common and familiar which arrived with contemporary "minimalist" literature offers a chastening example to those who would pursue new experience at any and all cost.

The focus on American writers here reflects not only my own American background, but also the nature of America as a place devoted to both self and new world creation (of course this too is a "tradition"). Lawrence is the lone non-American in these pages; and I take up his Mexican novel, his North American work. Poirier rightly identifies Lawrence, who figures strongly here, as being "by tempera-ment an 'American' writer" because, like Emerson and Whitman, he sought a style which "would release hitherto unexpressed dimensions of the self into space..." (37). Late modern texts of a romantic bent emphasize geography over psychology, cosmography over cosmology. Whitman is of course the key figure in regard to the romantic and American emphasis on self-exposure, especially in terms of imag-ining the self in geographical terms–as Manchild in the Promised Land. An enthnographic imperative runs throughout the works dis-cussed in these pages.

NeoRomantics seek to relandscape the derealized self by venturing outward; venturing outward they both empty and refurbish the self. Concomitantly, neoromantics tend to reject the general dispersion of self and flattening of experience found in Postmodernism, which reframes High Modernism in terms of deconstruction instead of construction yet primarily concerns itself, like High Modernism, with questions of language rather than self and experience. My emphasis is on an antinomian strain in modern American literature; my argument is that is a primary strain and one that infuses the second half of twentieth century in particular. And importantly, it is precisely by reaching a state of antinomian distance, and thereby coming to understand what Lawrence calls "the illusion of liberty," that neoromantics swerve toward a vision of some basic, even primitive version of community. By pursuing a new self or taking an extreme course–that is, the long way home–they come to an unexpected conclusion: they discover the illusion of liberty, of democracy, of self-agency, and thus the great truth of old orders, beneath Enlightenment or progressive traditions.

1

THE GREATER BODY: D.H. LAWRENCE'S
THE PLUMED SERPENT

In *The Plumed Serpent* D.H. Lawrence's desire for an open yet archaic-like form led him into new and strange territory–"novel" territory one might be inclined to say were it not for the fact it is as a "novel" that *The Plumed Serpent* has been most called into question. Critics who find a great deal to praise about the book are often forced to spend much of their time defending the novel's form from its detractors. L.D. Clark, for example, is keen to argue that many have misread the book because they were expecting a "novel" when in fact Lawrence's composition has more in common with the "romance" of classic American fiction than it does with the English novel.

My intention here is three-fold: to add my own comments to those who have traced Lawrence's models for *The Plumed Serpent*; to consider to what degree Lawrence's Mexican novel (or romance) anticipates postmodernist fiction; and finally, to briefly evaluate the success of the novel, especially in terms of its relationship to the high-modernist, symbolist novel.

Lawrence may be the key twentieth century writer in English in terms of both carrying forward nineteenth-century romanticism and influencing the development of a neoromantic or expressionistic postmodernism, which I distinguish from what many mean when they use the term "Postmodernism." I argue that to some extent we need to take *The Plumed Serpent* on its own terms: it is more utopian fiction than novel, that is, its dramatic and allegorical elements are foregrounded. This has the effect of setting up an abstract stage for the playing out of various ideas and desires. Lawrence's text is a pastoral (though somewhat violent) allegory in novel form. Its allegorical elements, along with the novel's playfulness, link the book to Postmodernism, especially the metafictional tendencies of "conventional" Postmodernism (for instance, Donald Barthelme's *The Dead Father*, discussed later, is an allegory of the fall of patriarchal society). It is of course the pastoral features of *The Plumed Serpent* that distinguish it from a good deal of conventional Postmodernism and tie the text to Romanticism.

These pastoral romantic elements, in combination with a certain expressionistic, action-packed playfulness, provide much of the book's color and, crucially, its vitality. In this vitality lies hope for the Novel as a form and for a postmodernism more attuned to the natural world and the life force.

All the World a Stage

I want to begin with the current scene (Clark's essay only leans in the direction of later twentieth century literature). Postmodernism, argues Ihab Hassan, cannot be defined by a single feature but rather through a constellation of features, many of which become evident because of their opposition to prominent high modernist and, to a lesser extent, avant-garde traits.

For instance, unlike High Modernism, which tends to be purposeful, hierarchical, and totalizing, Postmodernism tends to be playful, anarchical, and deconstructionist. While any text can be approached in a postmodern manner (Ulysses taught as a text that leads to a series of dead ends rather than as a master narrative), Hassan suggests further distinguishing features of postmodernism. Postmodernism is "far less aversive to the pop, electronic society of which it is part" than either modernism or the avant-garde. Postmodern books also tend to be "cooler" than the typical, politically-motivated avant-garde text, for example, Futurist, Surrealist, etc. (indicating the avant-garde's closer links to romanticism's rebelliousness). Yet like the avant-garde, postmodern works often seek to strongly test the social and political assumptions of the world, a world somewhat excluded from high modernist, late symbolist texts (259-271). Postmodern writers such as Donald Barthelme and Thomas Pynchon do not so much write novels as deconstructive entertainments, books that seek to once more open up the text to the big, dull, crazy, fun world beyond the borders of literary modernism.

One implication of postmodernism's open-endedness is a renewed sense of vista–of possibilities. The hopeful artist leaves things open and unfinished; he, or she, battles against being enclosed in a dead or reductive system; and often he approaches the world with a rueful sense of good humor, keeping himself ready for something that may arrive at a later date.

Susan Sontag believes Antonin Artaud is one the great figures of our times precisely because he tried everything and mastered nothing. Sontag quotes Artaud as delighting in "the disrepute into which all forms of art are successively falling" (30), while holding out hope for a master art to absorb all others.

In Postmodernism, the new is most likely to issue, if at all, at the most common levels. In "What Are You Doing After the Orgy?" Jean Baudrillard writes,

> How great it feels to disappear in the bosom of the masses! ... It is my fantasy to disappear into television's cold blue light, to disappear behind that screen, forever protected from it, because buried at the heart of this obscenity, blue also, sometimes black and white, I can lie in wait from the bottom of his silence for blinding signal of a definitive event. (46)

In other words, at a certain point conventionless life and art (conventional postmodern art)-- which finds both beauty and humor in the commonplaces of our existence–gives way to a view that envisions, however provisionally, some sort of "other" emerging from out of the void. An other-worldliness or mythopoeic aspect returns. If in our conscious lives we can believe in little beyond what we see before us, our unconscious insists on dreaming of other worlds, as Symbolism recognized.

Even a writer as rigorously self-erasing as Samuel Beckett cannot escape, and perhaps does not want to escape, hopes for renewal that naturally rise up when, as in *Worstward Ho,* the word "void" almost as easily registers a sense of something waiting to be filled as it does a sense of nothingness and waste. Indeed, much like Lawrence in *The Plumed Serpent,* Beckett's intention seems to be to provide a dramatic stage where words themselves, "simple" words–"Said," "Dim," "Void"– become complex characters that "contain" many meanings and where, more importantly, words begin to blur (by virtue of their position in a shifting syntax and their repetition) so that words once again acquire the attributes of pure sound, of chant. And since speech is, as Saussure argues, closer to "presence," all of Beckett's defacing and erasing strategies have the paradoxical effect of creating Being, a kind of purified and purer being, closer to the pristine world of first vision, first consciousness. *Worstward Ho* is a primer on the history of consciousness. The narrator of the book has seen too much, and thus his eyes film over. The result is a longing for original, pre-verbal creation. (Like many Irishmen, Beckett is a near-sentimentalist–sentimentality being something Richard Hugo says all great writers "risk".) But primarily it is not writers like Beckett, who apparently see their project as the unmaking and unmasking of inherited codes, who offer the most helpful clues for a necessary reanimation and revitalization of contemporary fiction. Fiction, especially the novel, requires a realistic base–often missing in Beckett–and missing to some degree in Lawrence's *The Plumed Serpent.* Moreover, fiction that relies too heavily on deconstructive tropes for its power will inevitably suffer from sterility, that is, the inability to provide something that lives, and lives as no other thing has before it. Barthelme's novel can be taken as a representative case. Despite Barthelme's creation of an interesting platform for the playing out of certain ideas and desires, the novel spends itself on characters, most especially the Dead Father, who have little vitality, who suffer from exhaustion. The Dead Father is the mythic father deposed. The father becomes a fallen God, as well as a clown and lecher (although in the best section of the book, "A Manual for Sons," he is also the heart-breaking father). This decentering of the father figure, and of individual consciousness itself, does indeed offer wonderful opportunities for bemused reflections on the state of the world and, as we shall see when we turn to *The Plumed Serpent,* such decentering of the ego is important to D.H. Lawrence's aims. But the flipside of this approach, for Lawrence as well as Barthelme, is that characters can appear to be little more than puppets the author drags around the stage. In order to fill the space, in the novel and in the world, "created" by God's absence, Barthelme becomes a ventriloquist, employing characters, foils, shades, projections, and images which are, primarily, the manifold voices of his own mind at the end of its tether.

Additionally, each voice, lacking an outside context, concentrates on the commonplace concrete, turning each commonplace thought or object or character into a kind of abstraction, thus creating an allegory of the everyday. Problems of meaning, value, and relationship become abstracted from social context, that is, the realistic base. While this condition of materialistic abstractedness is true to much of what we experience in contemporary life, and has led to new successes in literature, it does not mean that a novel can succeed by merely offering some mimetic sense of this state.

Lawrence identifies the heart of the problem in his comments on Paul Cezanne's still lifes and portraits:

> Sometimes Cezanne builds up a landscape essentially out of omissions. ... It is interesting in a repudiative fashion, but it is not the new thing. The appleyness, the intuition has gone. We have only the mental repudiation. [...] And the very fact that

we can reconstruct almost instantly a whole landscape from the few indications Cezanne gives, shows what a cliche the landscape is, how it exists already ready-made in our minds.... (581)

Such a mode and manner of composition lacks enduring interest: we have seen it all before and are left, rather unmercifully, to the limitations of our own cliche-ridden, disembodied minds. Roland Barthes makes a claim for omission: "Pleasure in pieces; language in pieces; culture in pieces. ... The text of bliss is absolutely intransitive" (51-52). Yet, in cutting through the dead weight of the monumental, we need, I believe, some trace of a new thing. Furthermore, this intransitiveness is especially detrimental to novel writing.

Other Worlds

There is another postmodern paradigm, less attached to popular culture, yet no less critical of the high modernist withdrawal to traditional Western values and sources, the result of High Modernism's despair over mass market values and pluralistic social structures. This other paradigm--neoromantic, expressionistic, ethnopoetic (and to some degree symbolist)-- seeks the renewal of modern culture beneath or behind contemporary Western orientations and seeks to realize this renewal in active life in addition to in art. In *Fantasia of the Unconscious*, Lawrence writes, "...some, like the Druids or Etruscans or Chaldeans or Amerindians or Chinese, refused to forget, but taught the old wisdom in its half-forgotten, symbolic forms. More or less forgotten, as knowledge: remembered as ritual, gesture, and myth-story" (55).

In Lawrence, perhaps especially in *The Plumed Serpent*, we see how this somewhat different approach–later taken up by such writers as Malcolm Lowry[1], Tennessee Williams, Charles Olson, and, the subject of next chapter of this text, Paul Bowles–first emerged from out the high art aestheticism of modernism. In "A Propos of Lady Chatterley's Lover," Lawrence writes, "We must plant ourselves again in the universe. ... It means a return to ancient forms. But we shall have to create these forms again, and it is more difficult than the preaching of an evangel.... The last three thousand years of mankind have been an excursion into ideals, bodilessness, and tragedy, and now the excursion is over" (*Phoenix* II, 510-511).

For Lawrence, high modernism was a shield against life; he believes there is a "greater body" behind and beyond attempts to restrict life and art to aesthetically satisfying categories. Lawrence holds in common with the postmodernists a desire to find artistic forms that breathe more freely. But he differs from conventional postmodernists in his fierce desire to locate a new being, one who carries all the power and wisdom of the ages, in particular pre-Christian ages. At his best Lawrence achieves an art not unlike this description of his from *Etruscan Places*: "The scene is natural as life, and yet it has a heavy archaic fullness of meaning" (64).

In *The Plumed Serpent* we slowly enter the kingdom of the men of Quetzalcoatl, a world where ritual, gesture, and myth-story supersede not only realist character and plot structures but also many of the formalistic conventions of high modernism, such as rigorous processes of aesthetic selection, totalization, synthesis, and sublimation. Lawrence didn't lose his ability to delineate character, develop a realistic plot, or achieve modernist sublimity when he left England (although some critics would have us believe so), rather he was faced with and embraced different challenges. Lawrence is following a path Edmund Wilson describes as being similar to Rimbaud's (Lawrence, of course, didn't give up literature), i.e., "...getting away to a life of pure action and a more primitive civilization" (283).

The notion of sublimation is key. Lawrence can be as smooth, as sublimated, as chromatically textured a writer as even Joyce when Lawrence so chooses. Witness this passage from *Women in Love*:

She wore no hat in the heated cafe, her loose, simple jumper was strung on a string round her neck. But it was made of rich yellow crepe-de chine, that hung heavily and softly from her young throat and her slender wrists. Her appearance was simple and complete, really beautiful, because of her regularity and form, her shiny yellow hair falling curved and level on either side of her head, her straight, small, softened features provoking in the slight fullness of their curves, her slender neck and the simple, rich-coloured smock hanging on her slender shoulders. She was very still, almost null, in her manner, apart and watchful. (57)

In this excerpt consonance and assonance, which Joyce often relied on, are skillfully employed, but for Lawrence the soft sweep of this slender woman is finally "almost null." The rich perfumes of the material world do not so much express vanity, as in much of Joyce, as nullity. The word "still" is especially resonant. Lawrence has drawn a "picture" of fashionable cafe society. Here, as elsewhere in Lawrence, an obsession with appearances, and more specifically, a desire to display ourselves in public, indicates an unhealthy ambition to maintain intact and unsullied our individual ego, to sublimate all that is not fitting and representative of our best self (Joyce beautifully renders just this problem of sublimation in his portrait of Gabriel in "The Dead").

There are scenes in *The Plumed Serpent*–in the "Tea-Party in Tlacolula," for instance–the equal of Lawrence's earlier work in terms of evoking the texture of modern life, but it is the desire to escape from the modern self almost entirely that distinguishes the book from the somewhat hermetic, self-absorbed works Wilson describes in *Axel's Castle*. Ironically, Lawrence flight from the self leads to the creation of a novel that seems, at times, little more than the author's wish-fantasies. Lawrence constructs a moated castle of his own. Extremes are closer than means. The flight from the self produces a self-enclosed world.

As an isolated modern individual, Kate Leslie, the protagonist of *The Plumed Serpent*, is described as having little or no significance. While visiting Mexico Kate gets caught up in a rhythmic dance that frees her (at least for that moment) from the terrible burden of her individuality, even to the point that she feels like a virgin again. "Men and women alike danced with faces lowered and expressionless, abstract, gone in the deep absorption of men into the greater manhood, women into the greater womanhood. It was sex, but the greater, not the lesser sex. The waters over the earth wheeling upon the waters under the earth, like an eagle silently wheeling above its own shadow" (143). Much of Lawrence's work is akin to a medieval tapestry, in which birds, animals, men, light, etc. each maintain their separate glow–instead of being sublimated to some single texture–and yet each can only be truly seen within the curves of the some living whole (which includes explication and abstract thought–though sometimes, in Lawrence, is too abstract). Lawrence writes,

> It is the appleyness of the portrait of Cezanne's wife that makes it so permanently interesting: the appleyness, which carries with it also the feeling of knowing the other side as well, the side you don't see, the hidden side of the moon. For the intuitive apperception of the apple is so *tangibly* aware of the apple that it is aware of it *all around*, not only the front. The eye sees only the front, and the mind, on the whole, is satisfied with fronts.
>
> But intuition needs all-roundedness, and instinct needs insideness. The true imagination is for ever curving to the other side, to the back of presented appearance. (*Phoenix* 579)

The style of *The Plumed Serpent*, the almost supersensory plunge into spirit of place, creates a landscape at once lustrous and mysterious, "real" and "unreal," or, to put it differently, "real" and "mythical." In a scene from the chapter "Marriage by Quetzalcoatl," for instance, we are provided with a powerful sense of living voices at the back of us– "the hidden side of the moon"--even though the scene, in its attention to modern dress, machines, etc., also creates a strong sense of the real, the present.

Kate waded slowly to the boat, and stepped in. The water was warm, but the wind was blowing with strong, electric heaviness. Kate quickly dried her feet and legs on her handkerchief, and pulled on her biscuit-coloured silk stockings and brown shoes.

> She sat looking back, at the lake-end, the desert of shingle, and the blowing, gauzy nets, and, beyond them, the black land with the green maize standing, a further fleecy green of trees, and the broken lane leading deep into the rows of old trees, where the soldiers from Jaramy were now riding away on the black horse and the donkey. On the right there was a ranch, too; a long, low black building and a cluster of black huts with tiled roofs, empty gardens with reed fences, clumps of banana and willow trees. All in the changeless, heavy light of the afternoon, the long lake reaching into invisibility, between unreal mountains. (357-358)

The scene continues: "Still the boat drifted. There was a smell of gasoline. The man pottered with the engine. The motor started again, only to stop again in a moment. (359) Here, as elsewhere in *The Plumed Serpent*, Lawrence's evocation of place, the site-specificity of the description, is designed to not only give a sense of a palpable present world but also to create a vivid possible world where intuitiveness has not atrophied.

Hymns, drums, and sermons are some of the different voices Lawrence employs to generate a realm where the daily rhythm of life is unlike modern, urban, white civilization, or, for that matter somewhat unlike the Mexican civilization Lawrence encountered in the early 1920's.

Although many have shown, most recently Ross Parmenter, the pains Lawrence took to make his novel of Mexico both authentic and convincing in terms of its temporal social context, clearly Lawrence also intended the book to serve extramundane and extra-literary purposes. Lawrence seems keen on providing a liturgy for a new religion. Parmenter writes,

> Lawrence also knew that every successful religion must have the equivalent of a Bible, with cosmogony, creation myths, a Savior, a cast of holy personages and ethical mandates, a hymnal, a Book of Common Prayer, and a collection of sermons, sacred images, a body of easily recognized visual symbols, and a repertoire of vestments, stances for praying at peak moments of worship, services for such occasions as marriage, burial, and ordination, each with its sacramental rituals, and regular services with established orders of procedures. (283)

Edwin Honig has described the age-old aim of the pastoral as a desire to "resurrect a lost paradise and invest it with new values" (164). The artificiality of *The Plumed Serpent,* the sort of ancient and epic stage set up in the novel, serves two primary purposes: a proscenium for the transfiguration of Ramon, Cipriano, and Kate into living gods of the new Quetzalcoatl church and a dias for the interpretive dialectics of the narrator of the book. And indeed these two aims are related, as Honig notes: "Dialectic transfer can be seen in allegory as the transvaluation of fictional agents from relatively static to progressively more active and meaningful roles in the course of the narrative. The dialectic transfer is effected when their ideational roles are fully tested in the action (the "drama") and finally resolved in the larger design of the allegory"(138).

Lawrence's appropriation of a foreign mythology allows him a certain degree of freeplay that the modernist novel, and perhaps more so the nineteenth-century English novel, would have discouraged. His pastoral allegory, his folk opera, is played out in a manner so wildly expressionistic (to detractors of the novel, in a manner of puerile wish-fantasies) that, despite the sometimes excessive and ponderous dialogue and general heavy-handedness of some scenes, Lawrence appears to be having fun.

This fun is similar to that found in postmodernism. In Lawrencean Mexico things happen, and they happen quickly, abruptly:

"Where is Don Cipriano?" she [Kate] asked.

"Don Cipriano is very much General Viedma at the moment," he [Ramon] replied. "Chasing rebels in the State of Colima."

"Will they be very hard to chase?"

"Probably not. Anyhow Cipriano will enjoy chasing them. He is Zapotec, and most of his men are Zapotecans, from the hills. They love chasing men who aren't."

"I wondered why he wasn't there on Sunday when you carried away the images," she said. "I think it was an awfully brave thing to do."

"Do you?" he laughed. "It wasn't. It's never half so brave, to carry something off, and destroy it, as to set a pulse beating."

"But you have to destroy those old things, first?"

"Those frowsty images–why, yes. But it's no good until you've got something else moving, from the inside". (319)

This talk of action (and of transformation) is interrupted by gunfire.

At that moment, he sat erect, listening. There had been a shot, which Kate had heard, but which she had hardly noticed; to her ears, it might have been a motor-car backfiring, or even a motor-boat.

Suddenly, a sharp little valley of shots.

Ramon rose swiftly, swift as a great cat, and slammed to the iron door at the top of the stairway, shooting the bars. (320)

Lawrence's fun in this passage takes at least three forms: the play of quick, arch dialogue (as well as the straight-forward humor of

Zapotecs chasing non-Zapotecs); the ironic humor Lawrence's enjoys at expense of modern Kate who thinks a gunshot might be a motor-car or motor-boat; and, perhaps most significantly, the fun of undercutting social dialogue with dramatic, and violent, action. Action, as well as of course the shift from some form of dialogue or description to action, became increasingly scarce in high modernist art, which tends to sublimate such action-oriented, mixed-up material.

Indeed, in "Indians and An Englishman," written just prior to beginning his work on *The Plumed Serpent*, Lawrence identifies the Southwest he encounters in the early twenties as being "like a stage," and thus "not like a proper world" (92). He writes, "It is rather like comic opera played with solemn intensity. All the wildness and woolliness and westernity and motor-cars and art and sage and savage are so mixed up..." (*Phoenix* 92). Lawrence is taken aback and yet thrilled by his encounters with Southwestern Navahos and Apaches:

> The gobble-gobble chuckle in the whoop surprised me in my very tissues. Then I got used to it, and could hear in it humanness, the playfulness, and then, beyond that, the mockery and the diabolical, pre-human, pine-tree fun of cutting dusky throats and letting the blood spurt out unconfined. ...the fun, the greatest man-fun. The war-whoop. (95)

Living Form

Many contemporary writers respond in ways similar to Lawrence: action and ritual action override morality and metaphysics. Consider this passage from T. Coraghessan Boyle's short story "Greasy Lake": "Before we could pin her to the hood of the car, our eyes masked with lust and greed and purest primal badness, a pair of headlights swung into the lot. There we were, dirty, bloody guilty, disassociated from humanity and civilization, the first of the Ur-crimes behind us..." (6). In postmodernity only a superficial narrative is employed, leaving room for the playing out of the spectacle, that is, individual scenes of excitement and sensation, primal in aspect.In the work of novelist and short story writer Barry Hannah, for instance, the narrative (as well as authorial comment and moral evaluation) is truncated, and thus his characters act outside of and in opposition to usual narrative injunctions (be good, work hard, stay in line, practice patience, etc.) Hannah's stories often thrust us into the middle of a violent and unassimiable situation. "Midnight and I'm Not Famous Yet" begins: "I was walking around Gon one night, and this C-man–I saw him open the window, and there was a girl in back of him, so I thought it was all right–peeled down on me and shot the back heel off my boot" (105). Violence in Hannah often serves as a means of getting closer to "raw" experience, even at times pastoral experiences. In an interview, Hannah discusses his novel *Ray*: "Flying a jet can make you feel all kinds of things. When Ray was taking about glory there ... he wasn't necessarily talking about violence. He did shoot up people over there [Vietnam]; he had to. But the glory he saw was mainly being in the air, being close to the stars" (113).

An unwillingness to sublimate performative, and specifically primitive, even puerile performative, aspects of one's desires is an especially postmodern (as well as avant-garde) attitude. Lawrence wants to move the novel back towards realms of popular culture, e.g., the historical novel, the exotic novel, the action-adventure story, etc. Lawrence is trying to apprehend, record, recreate (and enhance) the world he came across in Mexico. Ethnological projects–for example, James Agee's *Let Us Now Praise Famous Men*–require the transcription of various kinds of materials and experiences.

But a novel requires, to a greater degree than "nonfictional" ethnographic literature, a teleological structure, that is, an encompassing and forward-moving design. Lawrence's novel does cohere: the resurrection and reinvesting of the Quetzalcoatl church provides a social, dramatic, and metaphysical context, and Kate's debate over her role in the church yields dramatic tension grounded in the real life struggles of humanity.

This ground-situation mitigates against the natural tendency of allegory, itself a "popular form," to become static, ritualistic, and repetitive. Furthermore, the interpretive acts of the writer, his unwillingness to sublimate his metaphysic (even as he undercuts it and juxtaposes it with action) gives the novel a controlling voice–or, to put if differently, weaves the tapestry together. But (this is indeed a novel that provokes "buts" and "yets") there remains the question of the appleyness of *The Plumed Serpent.* Jose Ortega y Gasset writes,

> The "I" is the innermost being, it is that which is within us, it exists for itself. Nevertheless it must, without losing this innermost character, find a world which is fundamentally different from itself and go forth, outside itself, to that world. Therefore the "I" must be at once intimate and exotic, withdrawn and free, a prisoner and at liberty. The problem is startling (182).

This is the problem that faces Kate, as it faces Lawrence the novelist. In the last chapter of the novel, Kate thinks to herself: After all, when Cipriano touched her caressively, all her body flowered. That was the greater sex, that could fill all the world with lustre and which she dared not think about, its power was so much greater than her own will. But on the other hand, when she spread the wings of her own ego, and sent forth her own spirit, the world could look very wonderful to her, when she was alone. But after a while, the wonder faded, and a sort of jealous emptiness set in.

"I must have both," she said to herself. (481-482)

Lawrence, as writer, also tries to have both: a novel that charts the psychological and spiritual journey of a twentieth-century European, Kate, and a novel that responds to the ancient otherliness of Mexico. And perhaps one can not ever assimilate the materials and spirit of another culture as well as one can approach one's own culture and the other that lies beneath and behind it. "Lawrence, for all his rovings, must come back to the collieries again," writes Wilson (288). But, in the aftermath of World War I, Lawrence felt that England, and all of northern European culture, was dying, and beyond resuscitation.

The Plumed Serpent carries forward Lawrence's search, philosophically and artistically, for a new being, one that conveys the power and wisdom of pre-historical cultures. Much of the liveliness of the novel derives from the passionate nature and expression of Lawrence's yearnings. In the novel, at its best, ritual, gestures, and myth-stories are woven with the new toward the creation of the world.

But in the end Kate asks of this mythological kingdom, as we must ask of the novel, is the myth convincing? Is it mere fantasy, or at best thoughtful utopianism, or is it truly a living, breathing myth which curves round to "the back of presented appearance," so that we feel its appleyness? Does Lawrence's myth provide us with a sense of a possible world while acknowledging the nature of modern sensibilities? Does this myth of the men of Quetzalcoatl, and its attendant symbols–the morning star, the evening star, the dark sun, and the lake–contain, without silencing, the many voices of the earth. Does *The Plumed Serpent* have living form? And is it a good model for postmodern times?

It is not a wholly successful novel. At times it lacks certain novelistic virtues, such as ones mentioned earlier: character and plot development. Ramon and Cipriano are too much alike, even for brothers in Quetzalcoatl, and Kate does not so much develop as give in (only to partially retreat from embracing Quetzalcoatlism in the end). But a more serious limitation than insufficient character and plot development or the dearth of sublime, modernist symmetries (though, for instance, the return of the bull in the last chapter fittingly recalls the bullfight in Chapter I), is the lack of adequate response in the novel to modern life itself, with its black humor, friction, and urban beauty. What is especially missing is the world of business.

In the latter parts of the book the voices of the modern world are almost entirely displaced. Jerome Rothenberg describes contemporary poetics in terms of an art of "displacement: a poetry that transports us from where we are to where we might be" (591-592), and certainly Lawrence seeks these effects. Rothenberg writes,

> And metaphor–if that is what we have or think we have becomes *transformative,* envisioning, invoking, the strange and marvelous (that key word of the Surrealist fathers), 'causing to see'. ... From this kind of metaphoric language-making, the shamans and other native ritualist and singers go on to more structured and often more extended forms of visualization. (592)

But in a novel, in particular, the vision cannot be wholly other, for then the dramatic tension, the tension between life as it is and life as it might be, is lost.

The Plumed Serpent becomes too much a manual for living, not the living work of a man of his time. The novel too often seeks to make the new way of living too explicit. Cipriano says to his followers:

> "Are we men? Can we not get the second strength? Can we not? Have we lost it forever?
>
> "I say no! Quetzalcoatl is among us. I have found red Huitzilopochtli. The second strength!
>
> "When you walk or sit, when you work or lie down, when you eat or sleep, think of the second strength, that you must have it.
>
> "Be very quiet. It is shy as a bird in a dark tree.
>
> "Be very clean, clean in your bodies and your clothes. It is like a star, that will not shine in dirt.
>
> "Be very brave.... (398-399)

This passage, like others, sounds as if Lawrence were merely translating a foreign religious story into English. The didactic and humorless quality of much of the writing in the novel, especially as it progresses, brings into question his commitment to representing life as it is. Ironically, Lawrence's search for a more primal and truer mode of being led him to construct a world far removed, like much symbolist work, from much of what we experience in quotidian existence.

But my final interest here is not to evaluate *The Plumed Serpent* as a novel. Rather I seek to point out that we have in this novel, or romance, a vitality beyond even some of the best works of modern or postmodern genius, especially when their works are cut off from ancient sources of strength. Often in such cases the writer merely flails his (or her) own ego and ventriloquises his despair. The despair that caused Lawrence to turn his back on Northern Europe produced, in his case at least, a determination to find alternative ways of life. In *The Minoan Distance*, L.D. Clark writes,

> We realize, though we can seldom afford to face the fact and hope for gods to save us from it, that all we really know of the life force is that it seems to be composed equally of the will to create and the will to destroy; to create in order to destroy, to destroy in order to create again–the cycle of virginity and death. The ancient myths take account of this inexplicable course of existence, which goes its way oblivious to any morality we devise. The modern story knows no way to encompass it.
>
> In this respect, as in all others, *The Plumed Serpent* is Lawrence's bid to re-create a mythic consciousness out of America and a story form to create it. He fails, of course, for he is attempting a feat probably beyond the grasp of any modern writer. Still there is good reason to admire his boldness in striving for a form to reach a plane of experience that we know to be real enough still, even if we have lost the faculty for incorporating it into our conscious lives. (329-330)

In Lawrence, and in those postmodernists who have responded to his lead, we once more find traces, ghostly intimations of the return of the greater body.

2

QUEST AND PREDESTINATION IN PAUL BOWLES'S *THE SHELTERING SKY*

Luther voiced the spirit of this faith [Protestantism] when,
asked where he would stand if the church were to excommu-
nicate him, he is said to have replied, "Under the sky."

—*Huston Smith, The Religions of Man (348)*

Like Lawrence's *The Plumed Serpent* or Conrad's *Heart of Darkness*, Paul Bowles's *The Sheltering Sky* is a journey in which the central characters come face to face with heretofore unacknowledged truths about nature and the primitive self–dark, rueful truths that, paradoxically, perhaps offer a hope of renewal or salvation, even as they deny the possibility of regaining original innocence. For these dark revelations, while they emphasize the general brutality as well as indecipherability of the world, at the same time point to our common sinfulness and thus to the saving fact that we are all in this life together, for better or worse.

Bowles's novel is a journey, for both protagonists, Port and Kit Moresby, to the other side of the self, even to the other side of their respective sexes. In a sense, Port must become a woman and Kit a man. Only then are they sufficiently unmade as to reveal their common inheritance, especially in terms of the insufficiency of their former actions and their failure to look out for each other. But unfortunately, for their married life if perhaps not entirely for their individual salvation, Bowles's protagonists discover too late the indeterminate as well as brutal condition of both nature and human nature. In passing outside their own social realm, in entering alien lands, Bowles's characters, as he says in an interview, are at the mercy of "the Romantic fantasy of reaching a region of self-negation and thereby regaining a state of innocence" (Hibbard 149)–a desire in its born-againness and focus on individual salvation also Puritan and Protestant in origin.

The search for innocence, a kind of lost childhood, is inevitably vain. Yet, despite the fantastical element in the quest, the novel leaves unclear whether its protagonists could have come to understand the false promise of regaining original innocence in ways other than the extreme methods they followed, or were compelled to follow. It is as though the Moresbys' journey deep into the desert were predestined, either by unconscious compulsion or some supernatural force. When reading Bowles we sense something beyond immediate experience; there is a feeling of "ulteriority"–"beyond" in terms of "covert," as John Hollander defines ulteriority: an insistence on the prelapsarian meaning surviving in the fallen one (2). Along with our associating such covert feelings or longings with Romanticism, we may again also associate them with Protestant or Calvinist Christianity. As Thomas Bokenkotter writes: "In protest [against Catholicism] Calvin often insisted on God's absolute transcendence and total otherness, on his mysterious, incomprensible essence, his unfathomable purpose, and his inscrutable decrees. He was a hidden God" (239). Bowles, especially the forward, westering Port-side of Bowles–as well as the Kit who in some respects *becomes* Port in Book Three of the novel– searches for something absolute, abstract, sublime, and emblematic, and one might say *prelapsarian* in terms of its purity and unity.

To journey south–from the cold green Atlantic to the warm aquamarine Mediterranean–is to seek a ripe sensual landscape, a more various sexual and social latitude, and a more gracious, ancient (yet earthy) way of life. But to journey south beyond the Mediterranean into Africa and the Mideast is, for Bowles, to seek a more primitive and spiritual absolute beneath or beyond sensual, aesthetic communities; it is to pass through Catholic and pagan rites, through Dionysus and Apollo, through body and mind, ritual and word, even through female and male, to some sort of, at least in Bowles's work, Protestant/Oriental manifestation of the spirit. As in certain strains of Romanticism (a largely Protestant mode, and one often influenced by Oriental thought), matter is spiritualized. Yet one of the paradoxes of *The Sheltering Sky* is that the prelapsarian meaning is, apparently, the absence of transcendental meaning, the absence of God. The far frontier turns out to be a mirror, wherein nothing–although this is an important "nothing"–but the self is reflected. And for Bowles, the self is the seat of horror and depravity. Still, at that far point one may have replicated some redeeming aspects of the first American Puritans, the pilgrims: the Puritans were brave adventurers, and by going into the wilderness they came to understand the importance of social restrictions as a check against natural depravity. Furthermore, inside Bowles's world one is, like a Puritan, eternally watchful for signs or omens from God, that might come out of the nothingness.

Port and the Western Eye

In the novel an American couple crosses to a final frontier, one which they'd been going blindly toward for a long time, yet one they also seem little able to avoid and, on some level, have already experienced.[1] As the epigraph, by Eduardo Mallea, to Book One of in the novel suggests, Port and Kit appear to be acting out something predestined: "Each man's destiny is personal only insofar as it may happen to resemble what is already in his memory" (1). Such typological thinking is particularly Protestant and especially American, as Herbert Schneidau explains, "For Paul, Adam was a type (in the old sense of *image*, as in 'tintype' or 'Daguerrotype') of Christ, Hagar of the Law, and so forth. The Old Testament prefigures the New, the New fulfills the Old. The Puritans were zealous typologists, and ingrained this habit into the American literary imagination (154).

In *The Sheltering Sky* the Promised Land–this place registered deep in memory that waits for your arrival–is newly represented by the Sahara desert. And, in keeping with "the latent Puritanism in the Western heritage that urges us always to go upstream, nearer the source and therefore purer" (Schneidau 263), the Sahara, near the source of Western Civilization yet inhospitable to civilization, offers just about everything a Puritan might seek.

In Bowles, of New England heritage, the repressed Puritan heritage within Romantic Transcendentalism reappears in his stripped-down style–his desire to approach a place beyond words, where violence and solitude, sex and death, reign. Port is not even content with the International-Zone, post-World War II frontier of Morocco (as Lawrence Durrell's characters, for example, seem to accept, in somewhat dispirited fashion, the "international-zone" life offered by Alexandria).[2]

Rather, Port and the reluctant but soon converted Kit apparently feel compelled to journey into the heart of the Sahara, leaving behind, ultimately, the blue sea and sky of the Mediterranean for the blazing white daylight sun and sand and sheer black night of the desert. Wayne Pounds draws parallels between Edgar Allen Poe's *The Narrative of Arthur Gordon Pym* and Bowles's work. He quotes Edwin Fussell on Pym: "Symbolically, due South is the 'unknown,' the 'absolute,' or 'death'; allegorically, it is a displaced West" (11).[3]

Bowles, an only child of New England-bred parents, raised in largely upper middle-class, suburban New York, found in the Sahara a literal equivalent to the solitary and somewhat death-haunted world of his childhood, or at least of his childhood imagination. In keeping with American minimalism, Bowles scarcely explores his childhood past (except in his autobiography); yet one senses in his work, especially when we come to dream or drug sequences, the prelapsarian world of childhood lurking in the fallen adult world of the present.

Any sense of having "turned the corner" away from childhood, as he writes in "Call at Corazon," soon dissipates: the protagonist of the story, falling asleep one evening, finds himself "staring closely at a long-forgotten object–a plate, a chair, a pincushion–and the accustomed feeling of infinite futility and sadness [of childhood] would recur" (*Delicate Prey* 74).

Bowles's mother read Poe's stories to him when he was a child. In Bowles, as with Poe, the fallen world of the present seems to be but an extension of the fallen world of the past. The opening page of *The Sheltering Sky* describes Port as he wakes from a dream, disoriented, yet also in accustomed emotional territory: "He was somewhere, he had come back through vast regions from nowhere; there was the certitude of an infinite sadness at the core of his consciousness, but the sadness was reassuring, because it alone was familiar" (3).

Both Bowles and Poe were, or at least felt, deprived of most of the usual childhood pleasures; both appear to have felt condemned from the beginning–thus the sense that the depraved (yet spiritual?) end is contained in the beginning, or indeed prior to the beginning of one's own life, as in Calvinist predestination. Or, as Georges Bataille writes in the preface to *Story of the Eye*: "So much horror makes you predestined" (100). Port is haunted by dreams.

Yet commentators who see a kind of anticipation of the future in Bowles–Kit is haunted by omens–a writer ahead of his times, "proto-postmodernist" (Barth 114), are also right: despite an apparent attachment to present experience, registered by a minimalist style, Bowles's work slips beyond everydayness. The future and the (repressed) past link up as a way of warding off the commitments and terrors of the present. In "Here to Learn," from the story collection *Midnight Mass*, the protagonist thinks to herself: "The trees were going by very fast. It seemed to her that she had always known something strange like this would happen to her one day. It was a comforting thought, and it kept her from feeling actual fear" (49).

As suggested earlier, Bowles's protagonists are after something absolute, abstract, sublime, emblematic, and prelapsarian–that is, something that has the quality of dreams or childhood. Port responds strongly to the African setting:

Outside in the dust was the disorder of Africa, but for the first time without any visible sign of European influence, so that the scene had a purity which been lacking in the other towns, an unexpected quality of being complete which dissipated the feeling of chaos. Even Port, as they helped him out, noticed the unified aspect of the place. "It's wonderful here," he said, "what I can see of it anyway." (194)

Yet Kit's response to Port's statement undermines Paul's expressed desire for something "complete": "What you can see of it!" echoed Kit. "Is something wrong with your eyes?" (194) She also points to Port's weakened physical condition as well as a more general emotional and spiritual weakness that pervades the novel: physical and mental health mirror each other; delirium is a condition of body and soul. Yet we shouldn't miss that even as Kit queried Port, she "echoed" him.

For the first two-thirds of the novel, and in some sense for the entire novel, the central intelligence is Port. It is Port who drags Kit, and Tunner, their American traveling companion, out to Morocco in the first place. According to Michelle Green, in *The Dream at the End of the World: Paul Bowles and the Literary Renegades in Tangier,*

In the spring of 1932, Paul returned to eat opium in Tangier and watch the frenzied rites of religious brotherhoods in Fez; the next winter, he came back to steep himself in the austere beauty of the Sahara, where the sky had a life of its own. The experience was a "baptism of solitude," as he described it: "Once [a man] has been under the spell of the vast, luminous, silent country, no other place is quite strong enough for him, no other surroundings can provide the supremely satisfying sensation of existing in the midst of something that is absolute," he wrote. (5-6)

Port seeks out such inhuman or superhuman extremes of frenzied rites and silent solitude, of sensuality and asceticism (extremes being closer than means) as vehicles for discovering his identity and the nature of human identity itself. Indeed annihilation is often considered, especially for men, a means to achieve identity. As Camille Paglia writes, "The quest romance of the male sex is a war between identity and annihilation" (27).

In Bowles this quest is played out in terms strongly colored–not surprisingly–by his American roots. On one level the sought for is nothing more, nor less, than happiness and pleasure. In a study of Bowles, Lawrence D. Stewart writes, "And Morocco has become, especially in this century, another outpost of the American dream, colonized by Americans in exile" (1). Port and Kit, and in a different way, Tunner, seem to feel obligated to, American-fashion, act out the pursuit of happiness. Happiness is not to be found in the "sad colonial room(s) where each invocation of Europe was merely one more squalid touch, one more visible proof of isolation" (52), but rather "happiness, if there still was [is] any, existed elsewhere: In sequestered rooms that looked onto bright alleys where the cats gnawed fish-heads; in shaded cafes hung with reed matting, where the hashish smoke mingled with the fumes of mint from the hot tea; down on the docks, out at the edge of the sebkha in the tents...beyond the mountains in the great Sahara, in the endless regions that were all of Africa" (52). Happiness, for most Americans, is not to be found in the drawing-rooms, European or otherwise. Happiness, if one can call it that, is waiting at the frontier, in the wilderness, the future, the beyond–Americans are brutal in their willingness to dismember social convention and the past in order to make possible the next juncture. In a sense, Port goes out ahead of Paul, into the silent desert; whereas Paul Bowles is a writer, a recorder of the past, Port no longer writes: "And even if what he might have written had been good, how many people would have known it? It was all right to speed ahead into the desert leaving no trace" (207).

But at a certain point, the pursuit of happiness, the desire for new experiences and pleasures, becomes compulsive–pleasure has a way of establishing its own agenda. D. H. Lawrence's insight into the American psyche's pursuit of new, titillating experiences, which he finds especially apparent in the "intense vibrations" of Poe—and into the control, ultimately, that such a pursuit has over an individual is clearly applicable to Port, despite Port's apparent detachment. As he descends the streets of Oran toward a rendezvous with a young native prostitute, Port thinks to himself: "The odors in the air grew ever stronger. They were varied, but they all represented filth of one sort of another. This proximity with, as it were, a forbidden element, served to elate him. He abandoned himself to the perverse pleasure he found in continuing mechanically to put one foot in front of the other, even though he was quite clearly aware of his fatigue" (16).

Port thinks of turning around and going back, to where Kit waits for him (though even at that moment he is imagining her at his side, watching him), but he continues on somnambulantly, almost as though he is acting out a scene already established in the theater of his mind. Again the links to Poe are obvious. Lawrence writes that Poe "was an adventurer into vaults and cellars and horrible under-ground passages of the human soul. He sounded the horror and the warning of his own doom" (81). Bowles was a great admirer of Lawrence: "I've read all his things, with excitement for years" (Caponi, *Conversations* 48). And Bowles provides, as Lawrence almost always does but Poe often does not, an outside world, "Spirit of Place," the tang of a frontier experience, whatever the price to the adventurer. The compulsive nature of the sought-for new experiences turns all pleasure into pleasure/pain. The Orient is perhaps, at least in the mind of Westerners, a logical locale for such experiments. Lawrence Durrell writes, "The Orient cannot rejoice in the sweet anarchy of the body—for it has outstripped the body" (14). The Puritan may be after just such a state of being: to be stripped naked and defiled, and thus arrive at some point beyond bodily desire, however great the cost.

At any rate, the wandering Port must go to the ends of the earth to find himself. "The Western eye is a projectile into the beyond, that wilderness of the male condition" (Paglia 31). The opening sentence of the novel–"He awoke, opened his eyes." (3)–associates Port with sight, vision. To Kit's dismay, Port pours over maps:

> His wife watched the meticulous movements he made with amusement and exasperation; maps bored her, and he was always consulting them. Even during the short periods when their lives were stationary, which had been few enough since their marriage twelve years ago, he had only to see a map to begin studying it passionately, and then, often as not, he would begin to plan some new impossible trip which sometimes eventually became a reality. (6)

Port is the masculine, and perhaps colonial, imagination at work. Maps are representations of power and control; the colonialist is ever mapping out God's plan, God's land. But Port does not want simply to map the country from above, he does not want simply to control others, he wants to–or claims to want to–enter the horizontal plane of their existence. This means bringing himself down, at least to some degree, to the level of their daily experience. Yet this, too, may be foolhardy. Port can not live as the natives do, despite his protest that the world of the Sahara belongs to him as much as to anyone: "I feel that this town, this river, this sky, all belong to me as much as to them" (122). The fact that he sees things in terms of possession indicates a colonialist's perspective, one which undermines attempts to belong or make contact.

The Promised Land–which in Bowles is something of an illusion itself, a mere projection–can only be reached through an underworld or alternate-world journey, through degradation and even humiliation. One must be brought to one's knees. But Port can't really feel the reality of his degradation–can't really enjoy it?–unless Kit is looking on. He requires a witness. He likes to be watched. The observer/observed voyeuristic element of the novel, the kind of imaginary theater Bowles sets up, contributes to the allegorical quality of the book.

Again we are in a Puritan world. Alfred Kazin writes in *God and the American Writer,*

> In the beginning at New England our writers were Calvinists, absolutely sure of God and all His purposes. He created man to glorify Him forever. But never sure of his obedience, distrustful of his innate disposition to sin, God kept man forever under His eye. Each claimed to know the other because there was a covenant between them, a contract. Each was eternally watchful of the other, each apparently needed the other. (3)

The allegorical quality of the novel is also not unlike a quality Richard Tarnas associates with the postmodern mind: "The fate of human consciousness is ineluctably nomadic, a self-aware wandering through error" (399). That Port is self-aware is implicit in voyeurism. Port's journey toward otherness is, in some respects, nothing more than a journey into a mirror. Otherness is what he doesn't want! (though he is perhaps aware of that, too).

But not just any witness will do—only his other half, his alter ego, his wife, Kit. Kit must watch as Port displays his lusts, weaknesses, and fears; she must watch as he undermines whatever trust she might have in him and in their marriage. She must watch as Port displays his unmanliness, telling Tunner of a dream in which Port imagines having to live his life over again: "I couldn't face the idea of all those God-awful fears and pains again, *in detail*" (10).

Kit realizes, further, that Tunner will seize on this apparent lack of manly virtue, that is, an unwillingness or inability on Port's part to keep his soul separate and intact. She fears she will no longer be able to resist the handsome Tunner, or, after Port's display, have much reason to. It is, perhaps, a supreme irony of the novel that whenever Port displays his more emotional side—his "feminine" side—Kit is seemingly more alarmed than she is by his projecting and detached "masculine" side.[4] But it may be that Kit is reacting not so much to Port letting down his guard as she is to his need to display such emotions in front of Tunner.

Kit and the Dionysian Body

Point of view in *The Sheltering Sky* shifts back and forth between Port and Kit, with occasional shifts to Tunner, as well as various minor figures. The modern master of dual point of view, especially between male and female, is Lawrence; Malcolm Lowry also makes effective use of a shifting point of view between a husband and wife (and a third, the husband's brother) in *Under the Volcano*. Bowles, like Lawrence and Lowry, is primarily concerned in his work with relations between husbands and wives. *The Sheltering Sky* is one of the great twentieth century novels on marriage. (Indeed the general absence of great novels in postmodern times may be chiefly due to the diminution of the central role of marriage, the Ur narrative most crucial to novels, an essentially bourgeois form.)

For Port–and this may be his primary failing–marriage is something wherein you are together without actually being together in any highly emotional or sexual way. Port's emphasis on movement and solitude suggests a fear of involvement, and perhaps, to employ Paglia's terms, fears of the Dionysian, chthonian excesses of femaleness. These fears find a home in the Unconscious. Donna Caponi writes, "To the fastidious, compulsive Bowles, the unconscious was messy, gushy, and uncontrollable. Its dark fertility, that 'damp breeding place of ideas' he had discussed in *Let It Come Down*, was rich with the stuff of life–soil, mud, and blood–and death, and it repelled Bowles more than any force of nature ever terrified his wife" (211).

Bowles the writer is well aware of the "self-imposed" limitations of Bowles the man–the later visible, at least in certain respects, through the creation of the character Port. Port is "unable to break out of the cage into which he had shut himself, the cage he had built long ago to save himself from love" (100). The "long ago" suggests that Port's problems may have begun in childhood. Despite his having recognized a "glacial deadness," as the cause of his "unhappiness," Port clings "to it [the deadness] always, because it was also the core of his being, he had built the being around it" (145). For Kit, marriage is mostly about being together, of dependence: "It made her feel abject, and therefore, of course, furious with herself to realize that everything depended on him ..." (40). But Kit is little willing–and this may be her primary failing–to risk failure. She wants Port to come back to her, but is "far too intelligent to make the slightest effort in that direction herself; even the subtlest means would have failed and to fail would be far worse than never to have tried" (40). Or perhaps her unwillingness has an even more chilling source: Puritanism. Sherwood Anderson writes about such matters in a letter: "As though if we dared love and help each other we had in some way sinned. Is that Puritanism, I dunno" (604). Marriage, like society, should be a sheltering sky, but the refusal of emotional attachment on Port's part and the refusal of independence and solitude on Kit's part, and the lack of initiative on both of their parts when it comes to their relationship, prevents them from sheltering each other from the ravages of nature and fate.

Port lives not so much by symbols as signs. In wandering, signifier supersedes signified, reading the road map replaces meaning, surface replaces depth. One is kept in a state of suspension, which makes things ambiguous and ambivalent, allowing for various possibilities, including at times hope–as Kit, who also visualizes, suggests: "Against her will she forced herself to admit that she still belonged to Port, even though he did not come to claim her–and that she still lived in a world illumined by the distant light of a possible miracle: he might yet return to her" (40).

But generally Kit's visualizing does not tend toward Port's more Apollonian, masculine, transcendentalist manner; rather Kit visualizes dark catastrophes. In some respects, Kit is more the Calvinist than Port–and therefore more profound? If for Port there is nothing behind the sheltering sky–"Nothing ... Just darkness. Absolute night." (101)–for Kit it hides danger and evil. She could "feel doom hanging over her head like a low rain cloud" (37). The Sahara is a place for omens. As Huston Smith writes, prior to the coming of Islam, Arab belief took the form of an "animalistic polytheism, it peopled the desert with beastly sprites called jinn or demons" (219), fantastic personifications of the terrors of the desert. The seemingly infinite spaces of the Sahara portend something–something frightening, something repressed, but perhaps necessary to understand. Nelson Dyar, in *Let It Come Down*, experiences such fears (if little along the lines of understanding) when he ventures out into the desert:

> "To see infinity in a grain of sand." The line came to him across the empty years, from a classroom. Outside was the winter dusk, dirty snow lay in the empty lots; beyond, the traffic moved. And in the stifling room, overheated to bursting, everyone was waiting for the bell to ring, precisely to escape from the premonition of infinity that hung so ominously there in the air. The feeling he associated with the word *infinity* was one of physical horror. If only existence could be cut down to the pinpoint here and now, with no echoes reverberating from the past, no tinglings of expectation from time not yet arrived! (254-5)

Traditionally understood, to be or become feminine is to minimize visualizing, to move away from projection and introspection toward a level of immediacy and touch: Kit's omens are felt presences. The primacy of sight in the desert–the importance of light, the vast expanses, the unvarying landscape–is, when we come to Kit's central episode, in Book Three, increasingly replaced by touch, as in, of course, her heated sexual encounters with Belqassim and Amar. Even the visual landscape is altered; the sky catches fire, and sight and heat combine: "the entire sky was like a metal dome grown white with heat" (288). Increasingly, blue is replaced by white, and white by a charred red and black. Kit's skin is blackened by the sun: "She went to the camels and opened her bag for the first time, looked into the mirror on the inside of the lid, and discovered that with the heavy tan she had acquired during the past weeks she looked astonishingly like an Arab boy" (291).

Yet, if in some respects Kit outdoes Port–goes further and more deeply into the Arab world, pushes beyond sight to touch, contact–in other respects she merely becomes Port and lives out his desire for solitude and silence. Further, whatever sensual reawakening Kit experiences generally comes at the hands of those who will command her in ways she had formerly hoped Port would (but one gets the feeling he wants to watch as others, including Tunner, do it to her).

Kit in Book Three, after Port's death, appears to be a projection of Port's desires, even to the point of being a kind of ghostly projection of Port himself. Kit understands Port's desire for someone to love "solitude and the proximity to infinite things" as much as he does, and she understands his desire for her "to become as he was" as representing, perhaps, his only hope of finding "his way back to love" (99). Even though Kit seems to be reborn–sensually, at least–through her encounters with the Islamic men, she does not seem to have really escaped Port's influence. Just as Book One begins with Port awakening and opening his eyes, so Book Three begins with Kit opening her eyes. Again, a visual, and voyeuristic, link is established between them, as if now Port is watching her, perhaps like a God above, or as though she herself has now become Port–and forced to both be him, be a man, or boy, and watch him as he submits to the Arab men.

There is, indeed, a sense that Kit is something of a vehicle of exchange between not just Arab men, but Port and Arab men. When Kit is forced to submit to both Belqassim and his friend, she supposes "that it was a gentlemen's agreement, made for the duration of the voyage" (288). This, of course, not only suggests that Port might be said to stand in as "friend" but that Tunner might as well–and further, that Port and Tunner for the duration of their Sahara sojourn likewise have an unwritten though tacitly acknowledged "gentlemen's agreement" with regard to Kit.

Yet, as stated earlier, Port and Kit do need to cross over to each other in order to survive as a couple. To some degree, they even need to cross over to the other side of their respective genders. In coming to the East, Port may have instinctively sought out a culture which rejects visualizing in the sense that it is less attached to historical time (or has a less progress-oriented sense of historical time). As Dyar says in *Let It Come Down*, "[I]n order to feel alive a man must first cease to think of himself as being *on his way*. There must be a full stop, all objectives forgotten" (183).

Port perhaps senses that he must stop visualizing and become more feminine. While Amar warns Kit, "Women always think of what is finished instead of what is beginning" (323), Port perhaps needs to be more aware of things ending. The traditional idea that women are aware of love slipping away day by day and men only when a relationship is over–and it's too late to do anything about it–is relevant to Kit and Port. Port only truly discovers his love for Kit on his deathbed.

In the opposition and, to some extent, interplay of male and female lies salvation. But Port and Kit never, as Port says, "get all the way into life" (101), are never able to cross over to the other. Port cannot accept love and Kit cannot accept solitude. In order to become real, Port must be stopped–in time and place. He must give in, become more feminine, stop visualizing and simply live in the present. His masculine, Protestant, spirit-driven imagination must marry the feminine, non-Protestant, bodily imagination: Kit's pagan and Catholic willingness to get close to the Arabs, and especially Arab women, provide, if only he realized it, the resistance he needs (his encounters are merely sexual, colonialist). Only after Port's death, when Kit more or less becomes Port, or at least lives out Port's fantasy–perhaps making it somewhat her own in the process–do both masculine and feminine principles come fully into play, do both sight and touch become fully active.

Yet by then, as I've already argued, it is too late: not only is Port gone, but in a strange way Kit merges her personality with his, and merging is the way of dissolution and death. Indeed sight and touch, projection and immediacy, visualization and action, may be not so much integrated as confused; a kind of somnambulant repetition takes over: "She [Kit] did only the things she found herself already doing" (289).

As a reader progresses through the novel it all begins to seem weirder and darker than one might have first imagined, for the future events of the novel are, in some respects, already laid out, already predestined, as though the characters were merely acting out something already lodged in their memory or unconscious, or even something already predetermined by the impersonal laws of the universe. Kit remarks, when with the two Arab men, "Again she was happy for a while, floating on the surface of time, conscious of making gestures of love only after she had discovered herself in the act of making them. Since the beginning of all things each motion had been waiting to be born, and at last was coming into existence" (273). This sense of Calvinistic predestination, of things foreordained, is perhaps even to be found in the very process of the book's conception: "Bowles believed his book 'would write itself' once he had 'established the characters and spilled them out onto the North African scene,' and by the time he reached midtown Manhattan, he 'had made all the most important decisions about the novel'" (Caponi 124-25). Bowles moved back to Morocco with the idea of writing out this planned novel. The Muslim world he found there, with its "it is written" and "leave things to Allah" beliefs, no doubt fit well with his own inclinations and notions.

Early on in the novel, Kit, in order to feel at home with her omens, enters into a kind of complicity with darkness. She must do something wrong, something bad, something she will feel guilty about, so she sleeps with Tunner. After this adulterous act, and Port's death, which she may feel is related to her adultery, she punishes herself. Durrell writes in *Justine*: "Guilt always hurries towards its complement, punishment: only there does its satisfaction lie" (147-8). Kit thus submits to the Arab men. But in submission ("Allah" means submission) Kit finds both pleasure, that is, pleasure-pain, and her "identity."

It remains an open question whether Kit, as Port, could have achieved recognition of her depravity through other means than those she followed. She appears to be playing out expectations of both Port and some sort of watching god, as in a scene when Belqassim, her lover, shares her with another man: "She opened her eyes: the other man was standing above them, looking down on them" (273). By going into the recesses of the Arab world and then returning to the Western world, she is able to see herself, one of the damned, a man in the sight of God:

> Still she was convinced that this was the end, that it would not be long before they found her. They would stand her up before a great mirror, saying to her: "Look!" And she would be obliged to look, and then it would be all over. The dark dream would be shattered; the light of terror would be constant; a merciless beam would be turned upon her, the pain would be unendurable and endless. (323-4)

Romantic quest and Calvinistic predestination once more have found common expression.

NeoRomantic Art

Harold Rosenberg remarks that "lifting up a word and putting a space around it has been the conscious enterprise of serious French poetry since Baudelaire and Rimbaud" and goes on to associate Francophile John Ashbery with this attribute (qtd. in Donoghue ix). I would add Francophile Bowles, and add further that Bowles also participates in the Baudelaire/Poe French connection that shows how a certain kind of raciocination can lead to–if too rigorously applied–gothic (and Calvinist) horror. W.H. Auden writes,

> From Rimbaud down to Mr. Ashbery, an important school of modern poets has been concerned with the discovery that,

in childhood largely, in dreams and daydreams entirely, the imaginative life of the human individual stubbornly contin- ues to live by the old magical notions. Its world is of sacred images and ritual acts ... [Perloff's ellipsis] a numinous land- scape inhabited by demons and strange beasts. (qtd. in Perloff 250)

The bringing together of what we might label, once more, Apollonian and Dionysian strains is one of the great achievements of Bowles's work. Bowles takes a purity and simplicity of line and marries it to an impressionistic and often violently expressionistic use of color and sound. That such qualities appeal to Bowles is indicated by the fol- lowing first sentence of his translation of Isabelle Eberhardt's *The Oblivion Seekers*, stories and memoir set in the Muslim Near East and Africa: "Long and white, the road twists like a snake toward the far- off blue places, toward the bright edges of the earth" (19). The clean, minimalist, yet impressionistic description, wherein perspective and distance soften toward a mysterious, horizontal projection of self and landscape in conjunction, is a signature of Bowles's style, even in his translation work, as is some lurking "snake" or other creature. And throughout *The Sheltering Sky* Bowles makes heavy use of expressionist tools–sound as well as color. I am unaware of any writer who more consciously employs sound effects and sound motifs than the writer- composer Bowles. Sound, as Edvard Munch's *The Scream* suggests, is closest to primal agony. Yet Bowles also employs sound as a way of suggesting the theatrical nature of journey. Bowles, like Kerouac and other neoromantics, took existentialism on the road; and he, like Ker- ouac but to a greater degree, often suggest the traveling, grotesque theater troup aspect of the road show. A short exchange between Kit and Tunner must suffice here to make the point about sound effects.

There was a knock at the door into the hall.
"Oh, God, who is it?" Kit said aloud.

"Me." It was Tunner's voice. As usual, he sounded offensively chipper. "Are you awake?"

She scrambled about in the bed, making a loud noise that mingled sighs, flapping sheet, and creaking bedspring. "Not very," she groaned, at last.

There was a pointed silence, during which she remembered her resolution. In a martyred voice she called: "Just a minute, Tunner."

Interestingly, the French experience in the Near East, as described by Edward Said, is suggestive of Bowles's spare, elegant, yet haunting accomplishment: "Theirs was the Orient of memories, suggestive ruins, forgotten secrets, hidden correspondences, and an almost virtuosic style of being, an Orient whose highest literary forms would be found in Nerval and Flaubert, both of whose work was solidly fixed in an imaginative, unrealizable (except aesthetically) dimension..." (170).

The Sheltering Sky marks one of the high points of the neo-romantic novel, which includes such early figures as Lawrence, Andre Gide, and Ernest Hemingway and such later practitioners as Henry Miller, Jean Rhys, Lowry, and Graham Greene. Bowles wrote to a friend:

> The only difference I can see between the Romanticist and Neo-Romanticist is that besides not having had the Realist school from which to learn lessons (nor the Dadaist nor Surrealists) the Romantic having faith and hoping, wrote as though he had lost it, while the Neo-Romanticist having lost all hope and faith of the kind the Romantic had, makes his faith in his creations. But Jolas says the neo-romantic attitude toward life and art is doomed from the start because its aim is irrationalism. Be that or be it not, I should never be capable of holding any other than a romantic outlook. (*In Touch*)

Bowles mid-century work–NeoRomantic–comes after High Modernism and before yet near the beginnings of Postmodernism. In other words, *The Sheltering Sky* displays features of late-phase art– "accomplished but anxious"; "high classic form" defiled "with mother nature's sex and violence" (Paglia 99)–as well as anticipates aspects associated with Postmodernism, particularly in terms of its flattening of experience and its reflexive, voyeuristic, theatrical conundrums.

    The Sheltering Sky is both a fulfillment and refusal of Romanticism.[5] Quest and adventure suggest Romanticism, yet the Romantic susceptibility to exotic cruelty as an antidote to civilization (as in Lawrence's "The Princess" and "The Woman Who Rode Away") is played out in Bowles to no, or at least little, purpose or revelation–or to put it differently, we only learn by going where we have to go, but in Bowles we are not sure that we've learned anything except that we are compelled to go where we have to go. The final effect of *The Sheltering Sky* is something tending, like much mid-century work, toward the romantic and visionary, yet in Bowles's case also tending toward something restrained and empty, unnervingly so.

    Allen Hibbard quotes an excerpt from a Bowles notebook: "Since I am a product of C [Christian] society [New England-Unitarian forbears] I assume that I am to be counted among the Christians. If I am ever able to arrive at a point of view which expresses the Ch. ethos despite the corrosive effect [of] my own ignorance and weakness, I shall be supremely happy" (198). I'm not sure what Bowles means by Christian ethos–perhaps the injunction to love one another, and certainly Port and Kit could gain from acting on that command. Or perhaps Bowles has in mind what Day Slade argues in *Up Above the World*: "'The one thing Christianity has given the world is a lesson in empathy. Jesus's words are a *manual on the technique of putting yourself in the other's place* "(62). The titles of all of Bowles's novels–even *The Spider's House*–point to the sky, to the heavens, we might say. At any rate, one arresting effect of *The Sheltering Sky* is to give sensuous form, at once real and ethereal, embodied and disembodied, to the common philosophical notions behind Calvinistic predestination and Romantic quest.

That *The Sheltering Sky* does not offer a vision of transcendence, nor much in terms of a possible social compact, even "a solitude of two," to quote Graham Hough on romanticism (9), is perhaps disheartening. In the closing lines of the novel Kit, half-mad, half-reborn, back in Oran yet in limbo between two cultures, avoids a reunion with Tunner by fleeing. She hops on a street car and disappears: "At the edge of the Arab quarter the car, still loaded with people, made a wide U-turn and stopped; it was the end of the line." My guess is that Kit will be living, like Bowles himself, at the edge of the Arab quarter. And that unless she actually lives among the Arabs not just at the edge of them, and among them instead of as one of them–she will have failed. Ironically, it is the practical, none-too-deep Tunner not the overheated Moresbys who appears to come to some sort of friendly accomodation with the desert and the various people, Arab and French, inhabiting it. To remain a Western colonialist is to be half-hearted; to try to become an Arab is folly, Bowles appears to suggest. Yet Port and Kit are, tragically, so constituted that they have no other choice but to pursue their own methods.

3

SELF-PORTRAITS IN SPACE AND TIME: ROBERT LOWELL AND JOHN ASHBERY

The American century has passed and our country's writers are increasingly postmodern, that is, they continue to unmask temporal and territorial claims to national, regional, and even individual identity. However much a writer may seek to embody regional and American ideals, the changing world order and evolving notions concerning the inability of language to locate and authorize a subject encourages writers to see across distances and borders. But indeed, ever since Walt Whitman, this has been a central project of American writing, of American poetry especially. One of the ironies of American grain or the American sublime traditions, that is, the experimental, New York-based traditions of Whitman, William Carlos Williams, Hart Crane, and Wallace Stevens—and Paul Bowles—which Robert Lowell, for one, somewhat resisted prior to *Life Studies*, is that in the pursuit of freedom, vista, and a kind of transcendental all-inclusiveness (America is all countries merged and each individual American contains all), they dissolve, to a surprising degree, not only regions but "America." What remains is America as commitment to the open road or the new word, or, in more solipsistic formulations, as a mere projection and mirror of the self. Tenney Nathanson describes this double effect of

Whitman, the chief proponent of American "Democratic Vistas": "... speaking from its particular time and place, this [Whitman's] presence seems also to transcend it, projecting itself through intervals of time, as well as space, it thereby annuls" (5). Thus it follows that a late modern/ postmodern poet such as John Ashbery, who disperses rather than concentrates subjectivity (until, paradoxically, everything is the self) stands as a truer inheritor of the central American tradition than such city- state regionalists as Lowell, or, to take other examples, Lowell's fellow New Englanders, Edwin Arlington Robinson and Robert Frost, and Lowell's mentor, Southerner Allen Tate--formalists all. Yet Lowell's harried pursuit of the historical self, as a result in part of his unique position as a "Lowell," leads ultimately to a kind of "Double Dreaming" (to borrow the title of one of Ashbery's books), or "Double-Vision" (to borrow from Lowell's late book, *The Dolphin*), in which the emphasis falls less on the self that acts in historical time than on the self that defines or constructs a self or selves.

Robert Lowell is perhaps the last major nation-state poet America will ever have. As a product of an important literary family of New England, a region of the country which maintains an especially strong historical sense, Lowell employs history in his poems in ways we are not likely to encounter again. Yet in Lowell the crisis of the national idea, or ideal, finds a rich and agonizing portrayal, *linking* him to Whitman–that is, to the side of Whitman less concerned with universal consciousness–the self everywhere–and more to the side of Whitman concerned with the relation between the personal self and the representative, social American self. Lowell offers, in ways Ashbery generally cannot or doesn't care to, powerful visions of American culture in distress, which includes in a special way his own New England. Ashbery's work tends to be "post-apocalyptic": the best and worst of times have already happened, and, importantly, we must now live, for better or worse, on a flat earth mirrored by a flat sky, with but a hologram of the self in the air between. Or as Ashbery puts it in *Flow Chart*:

and so get over feeling oppressed, so as to be able to construct the small song, our prayer at the center of whatever void we may be living in: a romantic, nocturnal that must sooner or later go away. At that point we'll have lived, and the having done so would be a passport to a permanent, adjacent future, the adult equivalent of innocence in a child, or lost sweetness in a remembered fruit: something to tell time by. (76)

But in Lowell's work, especially the middle works, *Life Studies* and *For the Union Dead*, the crucible of "the times," as well as time as both a philosophical construct and a personal quagmire, is central to notions of self and representative self. Indeed Lowell is even a more politically-oriented writer than Whitman due to Lowell's Puritan conscience (which also informs both Lawrence and Bowles's work). Feeling oppressed and fighting oppression are live concerns in Lowell's work.

> These are the tranquillized *Fifties*,
> and I am forty. Ought I regret my seedtime?
> I was a fire-breathing Catholic C.O.,
> and made my manic statement,
> telling off the state and president,
> sat waiting sentence in the bull pen
> beside a Negro boy with curlicues
> of marijuana in his hair.

> ("Memories of West Street and Lepke")

The self-altering, self-questioning side of the project complicates Lowell's pursuit of moral history. When Lowell begins to question language's ability to represent self and self-in- society, as he does increasingly from *Life Studies* forward, he more fully enters the Whitman- Williams-Crane-Stevens-Ashbery world of a poetry of consciousness itself. Paradoxically, history leads Lowell away from historical or factual reality. In *Life Studies*, and particularly in *For the Union Dead*, the latter a focus of this study, Lowell moves past the regionalist, city-state tradition (the "nation-state" tradition), which tends to emphasize village life and morality–as in such early Lowell poems as "The Quaker Graveyard in Nantucket" and "After the Surprising Conversions"– toward the American-grain or sublime traditions, which tend to emphasize consciousness and indeterminacy. Lowell's poetry becomes both more personal and more public, and the lines between the two are blurred, while middle ground is excluded. However much Lowell gains from this change–*Life Studies* and *For the Union Dead* are his greatest works, and there is much to admire in *The Dolphin* and especially *Day by Day*–in the end there are also losses for Lowell and American poetry. The texture of local habitation begins to disappear in both.

New Yorker Ashbery emerges as perhaps the finest poet of the central if a somewhat diminished and attenuated American poetry tradition of experiment. Rather than tying his world to some idea of history or behavior, Ashbery's characteristic voice, a kind of circulating energy, resists locating itself in anything except the process of thinking/ writing/ living–Whitmanesque in its ongoing and extensive energy and Stevensian in its abstractness. Memories and nostalgia provide a semblance of a locus, as well as pathos–the lost worlds of farm and New York, of love and metaphor are poignantly evoked–but those memories "belong" to a different self (rather than just a strange or estranged aspect of one's self) or, more accurately perhaps, belong to another, different context.

Lowell's Life in Progress

"The life-in-progress of the protean poet, as representative of his time and place," as Richard Gray (256) describes Lowell's project, is in line with the side of Whitman which seeks the localized American epic. But Lowell tends, despite his intentions to embrace America, to build a wall between himself and his native country, even as he seeks to come to terms with it (Whitman's over-identification with others creates, as D.H. Lawrence argued, a different kind of obstacle in terms of his relation to his native country or people[1]). Lowell's fear of America appears to derive from a concern about being appropriated by American history, especially with regard to both the New England tradition and his own famous family heritage.

It is his mother's ambitions as much as his father's failures that Lowell fears. Indeed his father's failure to fit-in, as described in "Commander Lowell, 1887-1950," is offered as a somewhat hopeful sign.

The commander's son, Robert, describes a world that is tight-lipped and awful—class and gender restrictive. "There were no undesirables or girls in my set,/ when I was a boy at Mattapoisett--/ only Mother, still her Father's daughter." The flattening effect of the end-rhyme, "set" and "Mattapoisett," the rhyme being a mere repetition of the same sound, sets up a world closed and dull, and yet also ajar: single repetitions neither rise to the enlivening plane of ritual and dance, nor does this repeated sound click shut like exact rhyme (two different words meeting and matching at their vowels), nor leave open possibilities of new combinations in the manner of half-rhyme. The third line of the poem, "only Mother, still her Father's daughter," further establishes a world clotted and constricted, the similarity of the sounds "Mother," "Father's," "daughter," creating the sense of an odd conflation of roles, the word "still" contributing a sense of both stasis and eternal reoccurrence.

His father, we soon realize, is perhaps one of those "undesirables"; his claims to Robert's mother appear to be overridden by her own father. "Her voice was still electric/ with a hysterical, unmarried panic. "The territory is unreal and slippery, despite or rather because the rules are strictly laid down. Who is an undesirable? And further, the careful distinction between undesirables and girls is smudged, "undesirables" leaks into "girls" despite the "or," for both the former and latter are absent. The only girl allowed in appears to be Robert's mother—her girlness established by reference to her being a daughter. Apparently Robert cannot have other girls.

Significantly, "Commander Lowell" has begun with Mrs. Lowell. The second stanza shifts the focus from mother and son to father and son.

Having a naval officer
for my Father was nothing to shout
about to the summer colony at "Matt."
He wasn't at all "serious,"
when he showed up on the golf course,
wearing a blue serge jacket and numbly cut
white ducks he'd bought
at a Pearl Harbor commissariat...
and took four shots with his putter to sink his putt.

The "numbly cut white ducks" is almost too much to bear–one wants to turn away, sight and sound so deftly linked, almost to the point of doggerel! His father isn't hip; trained as an engineer, an Annapolis man, he is liable to show up at the golf course in a soiled white shirt and plaid pants, ever "cheerful" but somewhat friendless–"Cheerful and cowed/among the seadogs at the Sunday yacht club, he was never one of the crowd." He is given to "piker speculations!", but it is the failure to fit-in more than failure itself that Lowell is pointing to, and paradoxically, this failure to fit-in is strangely admirable, as is his father's "defiant" optimism. The fact that "In three years/ he squandered sixty thousand dollars" is not easily dismissed, but it also registers the presence of an independent, if foolhardy and somewhat childish man–and not incidently, one who escapes from a world where the only "girl," the only dominant female influence, is Mrs. Lowell. Commander Lowell belongs to a different time and place–a different subset–than the Mattapoisett of Robert's youth, and thus we see the importance of placing the dates, "1887- 1950," in the title. Under different circumstances at a different time Mr. Lowell might have been quite successful indeed, as is indicated at the end of the poem: "And once/ nineteen, the youngest ensign in his class,/ he was 'the old man' of a gunboat on the Yangtze." The themes of youth and age, especially in terms of the ill-defined distinctions between child and adult, beginner and authority figure are repeated, and made both immediate and historical ("Year after year"), as a way of pointing to the confusion and overdetermination of Robert's socialization and education; the temporalizing process also points toward Robert's later ability to understand, at least to some degree, the anachronistic position his father occupied. When Robert's mother reads to him from a book about Napoleon, we see how this process works.

> Long-nosed Marie Louise
> Hapsburg in the frontispiece
> had a downright Boston bashfulness;
> where she grovelled to Bonaparte, who scratched his navel,
> and bolted his food–just my seven years tall!

There is too much in those lines to parse adequately--which of course is why only a poem, and a rather telegraphic one at that, suffices for Lowell, who abandoned his autobiography--but one general sense of these lines is of a boy standing eye-to-eye with a soldier, Bonaparte, who resembles Lowell's father in terms of uncouthness, one-time success, and ultimate failure.

Uncomfortably to us, readers of the poem, Marie Louise Hapsburg, associated with Robert's mother by virtue of her "Boston bashfulness," grovels to Bonaparte, who in the last line is not so much Mr. Lowell but his replacement, Robert. To some extent Robert never recovers from being placed in such an unenviable situation, taking over for his father as husband and soldier. In addition to the prescribed (proscribed!), overdetermined nature of his cultural and family background, Lowell, in *Life Studies* and *For the Union Dead*, appears to fear the onset of middle age itself, the loss of youth and prowess, especially in a country which prizes them. His anxieties, however, fuel his powerful self-portrait of a contemporary American (if not always so successfully the creation of a more universal American epic); one often feels that in Lowell, as Emerson wrote in "History," "the crises of his life refer to national crises."

Lowell's own life becomes the chief subject of his work. But the life of Lowell, as a poet, and of Lowell, as one of the famous Lowell poets, means that the personal takes on an especially public cast (Henry Adams's "third-person"*Autobiography* also mines this territory of famous family Self as Other). From the moment he was born a Lowell, his psychological self was public space. And vice versa, exterior events, especially those with large scale public and historic implications, are particularly relevant to his psychological health. Furthermore, poetic utterance in itself leads in the direction of public life, especially in modern times when poetry is often read in public, as Lowell was often called on to do. And finally, Lowell is representing not only himself, and his singular family heritage, but also the historic civic orientations of New England.

His sense of selfhood is publicly determined to a degree far beyond average. The extent to which his life is bound up with history, and in particular literary history, is obviously disconcerting--if also of great value–to the writer. In "To Delmore Schwartz," for example, the speaker's sense of self seems overdetermined, somewhat comically, as he himself realizes, by historical and literary reference, from T.S. Eliot to Harvard to Joyce and Freud to Stalin.

In Lowell, self and history, including personal history, wrestle each other, and finally collapse into one rather static, dreamlike–often nightmarish–scene: the self, lacking self- authorized agency, cannot awake from history, cannot even separate out self and history. Efforts to overcome historical necessities only serve to emphasize the limits of the self as well as how meshed self and history are, especially if one is a Lowell. "Middle Age," the third poem in *For the Union Dead*, is illustrative of this intertwining of self and history in Lowell and of its unnerving implications. I reproduce it below in its entirety.

Middle Age

Now the midwinter grind
is on me, New York
drills through my nerves
as I walk
the chewed-up streets.

At forty-five,
what next, what next?
At every corner,
I meet my Father,
my age, still alive.
Father, forgive me
my injuries,
as I forgive
those I
have injured!

You never climbed
Mount Sion, yet left
dinosaur
death-steps on the crust,
where I must walk.

The disconcerting, uncanny moment of meeting one's own father (and Father as in God) on every corner as a version of one's self brings the movement of the poem, the dialectic of self and "Middle Age," to a sort of halt, a moment of stasis, "still," and yet pulsing, "alive"–and rather horrifyingly, "still alive," as if his father had risen from the dead.[2] The last stanza furthers the multitemporal weirdness: Lowell is following his father's footsteps to the grave, via the streets he, the son, is presently walking, simultaneously New York's and Mount

Sion's. In "Middle Age," the Father has already been there before, thus a sense of fatality, prolepsis, curtailment ensues. History is seen not as ground for movement and action but, as alluded to earlier, as a site for the Eternal Return of the same story.

There are some similarities to Ashbery's work here. The speaker in "Self-Portrait in a Convex Mirror" laments the general lack of fresh experience–"The fertile/ Thought-associations that until now came/ So easily, appear no more, or rarely"–and feels life's potent immediacy ebb: "To be serious only about sex/ Is perhaps one way, but the sands are hissing/ As they approach the big slide/ Into what happened. This past/ is now here." Also like Ashbery, the site of Lowell's "Middle Age" is somewhat post-apocalyptic, flattened, as we find in other Lowell images of that period, such as the "commercial photograph" of Hiroshima and the TV pictures of the "drained faces of Negro school-children" in "For the Union Dead." Lowell's later volume *History* is even flatter, emptier. Ashbery writes in "Self-Portrait": "The balloon pops, the attention/ Turns dully away. Clouds/ In the puddle stir up into sawtoothed fragments./ I think of the friends/ Who came to see me, of what yesterday/ Was like." But Ashbery's characteristic response to such return-experiences or meta-experiences is to embrace the uncharted present moment and movement, as in the following passage from "Grand Galop": "I cannot decide in which direction to walk/ But this doesn't matter to me, and I might as well/ Decide to climb a mountain (it looks almost flat)/ As decide to go home "Lowell, on the other hand, "must walk" streets of death and ghosts. In Ashbery, there is, if not a new world in the offing, at least a new context, a new day; but in Lowell, the concavity of experience tends to swallow up identity.

In "For the Union Dead," for example, the wavering light of a fish tank, the poem's central figure, infuses the poem with a gothic, cavelike atmosphere. Lowell recalls, from his youth, pressing his nose to the glass and looking in at the fish of the "old South Boston Aquarium," which has since been boarded up, but by the end of the poem one gets the sense that the world itself is a fish tank (which he looks in at or out from?), as "giant finned cars nose forward like fish."

Again, like Ashbery's "Self-Portrait in a Convex Mirror," reflective images, and the illusory, dreamlike qualities created by them--indeed the aquarium glass is *convex*--predominate in Lowell's poem, and in the whole of the sequence that makes up *For the Union Dead*. But whereas Ashbery's world is generally bright, mirroring, and holographic, though somewhat less so in "Self-Portrait," his greatest poem, Lowell's tends to be dark, opaque, spectral, phosphorescent.

Sooty, too. His world is dry, as in dust to dust, ashes into ashes (or, elsewhere, dry as a failed marriage). In "Water," the volume's opening poem, the water is too cold, but later, in "For the Union Dead," the closing poem, "the airy tanks" of the aquarium "are dry." The monument to Colonel Shaw and Negro infantry sticks dryly "like a fishbone/ in the city's throat." Those "giant finned cars nose forward" but not in water, in "grease." "Parking spaces luxuriate like civic sandpiles." In another poem from the same volume, "The Public Garden," the "park is drying./ Dead leaves thicken to a ball/ inside the basin of a fountain, where/ the heads of four stone lions stare and suck on empty faucets."

The public garden, the civic commons, and more generally, Atlantic culture are pictured as drained, empty--or, as in "The Mouth of the Hudson," polluted: "Chemical air/ sweeps in from New Jersey." Lowell himself is not the man he once was or would hope to be because, for one thing, he realizes he is representative of this dry (middle-aged? Medieval?) culture. There is a perverse logic here. He is a son of that culture, but also, as we have seen, he is father to it as well, for he sees himself as his father (Father) and as a father: "Father, forgive me/ my injuries,/ as I forgive/ those I/ have injured!" This complex, enjambed formula makes everybody parent and child to everyone else. One guesses that Lowell might be inclined to exclaim, "God help me," were it not so problematical, for he might wind up only talking to himself. In "Skunk Hour," his famous lines, "I myself am hell;/ nobody's here--," raise just such a tragicomic possibility.

Steven Gould Axelrod writes that in *For the Union Dead* Lowell made his own sense of "'witheredness'" his poetic subject, and that this witheredness is "as much cultural as it is individual" (137). Axelrod continues: "Much more than in *Life Studies*, Lowell's new volume reflects the politics of its time. In *For the Union Dead* Lowell reveals to us the struggle of an individual to bear the double burden of his existence, social as well as personal. His point is that public and private worlds are interconnected, each affecting and being affected by the other" (138). And further: "...Lowell exposed the private and public confusions he had undergone firsthand. Out of the wealth and poverty of his own experience he created his poetry of consciousness" (139). Recognition of this double burden of self and self-in-society, and of their interconnectedness, leads to a wider–if perhaps less free and active–consciousness; and perhaps more importantly, it leads to a focus on consciousness itself. Indeed, it is this mixing and merging of self and history which leads to a generalized smudging of the borders between self and other in Lowell, and to an increasing recognition of not just the (self) expressive qualities of language, especially poetic language, but also its power to undermine subjectivity. This dispersion of subjectivity can lead to questions about one's ability to identify what one truly believes in or holds on to as central. Writes David Kalstone of Lowell and "For the Union Dead": "The forceful suggestion in Lowell's poetry is that, in the face of history" no "clarification and [personal] resolve is possible; we takes our places among the ruins of time" (130). Yet Lowell seems to imply, especially in *History*, that there are rewards to be found in this more extensive, dispersed, and passive subjectivity. Axelrod writes that in the final poem in *History*, "End of the Year," Lowell superimposes the image of his art–his marked-up carbon paper (his Rosetta stone)–upon the image of deepening night:"bright sky, bright sky, carbon scarred with ciphers."

In the joining of inexplicable world and language, in the transformation of his world into language, Lowell finds his sustaining though ambiguous value. His words become stars, "scarred" but "bright." (211)

Ashbery's response to art-making may be even a little more ambiguous than Lowell's–the moment of recognition and expression, especially when codified in written language, is also precisely the moment when the thing noticed passes out of the present and becomes something else. Indeed Ashbery argues that the process of acknowledging a certain lucid apprehension of the world sunders and distorts that apprehension:

> *This* thing, the mute, undivided present,
> Has the justification of logic, which
> In this instance isn't a bad thing
> Or wouldn't be, if the way of telling
> Didn't somehow intrude, twisting the end result
> Into a caricature of itself. This always
> Happens, as in the game where
> A whispered phrase passed around the room
> Ends up as something completely different.
> ("Self-Portrait in a Convex Mirror")

Yet, paradoxically, the recognition that things become something completely different than we expected or planned may also lead us back to humanity, to people, if not exactly to the People, the Republic.

Ashbery's Cartography

As Keith Cohen points out in reference to Ashbery's use of a variety of discourses--the borrowing of phrases and cliches, the mixing of high and low diction--one of his aims is to dislocate and thus disman-tle "bourgeois" history; but Frederic Jameson's distinction between postmodern pastiche and modernist parody helps make clear the dif-ference between Ashbery and modernists (say, from James Joyce to Lowell) who, however much they dismantle, also acknowledge the availability of a true, or truer, discourse. For instance, the mannerist presentation of that ultimate mannerist Gabriel Conroy, in Joyce's "The Dead," goes a long way toward dismantling false discourses of family, nation, and religion in turn of the century Irish society, but in the end parody and irony are not applied to Gretta Conroy's love for the young Michael Furey.[3] In dealing with similar material, Ashbery would perhaps not parody it, but my guess is that he would just include it, pastiche fashion, without directly memorializing or privileging it, or, if he did privilege it–certainly we feel the pull of nostalgia in Ashbery--the gesture itself would be somewhat undercut, a la mannerism.

The central work of mid-century, of late moderns, of which Lowell stands as a major representative, is different from not only Ashbery and the postmodern world he leans toward, but also from that of the high moderns. Irony and parody, and pastiche, are minimized in late modern work and the need to reestablish a regional/national culture–"*For* the Union Dead," says Lowell (my emphasis)–is more apparent. Poetry, and prose as well, becomes more civic-minded, as seen variously in the work of Allen Ginsburg, William Stafford, and Adrienne Rich, to name but three mid-century poets. Perhaps literary history could be graphed as "descending" from God to King to Nation to Self to Language. If so, Lowell may be said to come toward the end of the Nation- Self period and Ashbery near the beginning of the Self-Language period, with World War II the dividing line, perhaps. However my scheme has limited applicability: for Joyce and other high moderns seem more properly Nation-Language writers, or perhaps International-Language writers, with the self somewhat submerged.[4] One of the interesting aspects of Ashbery's work is that he seems to be carrying on a dialogue with many traditions without adhering to any one in particular. Particularly disconcerting, if also engaging, is his use of a high style to write about everyday (yet crucial?) events. His work is as open to the lyric as to the discursive, to public idioms as to inner musings, to high philosophy as to pop culture. And yet I think we can profitably identify this openness as not just Ashberian, but as part of a larger trend in contemporary poetry, a postmodern poetry, a "post-nation-state poetry," of which Ashbery is perhaps the leading figure. This poetic mode is unintentionally but deftly described by Robert B. Kaplan in an article about the collapse of nation-states in the contemporary political world. The "map of the future," says Kaplan, will be like "cartography in three dimensions, as if in a hologram" (75). He continues:

> In this hologram would be the overlapping sediments of group and other identities atop the merely two-dimensional color markings of city-states and the remaining nations, themselves confused in places by shadowy tentacles, hovering overhead, indicating the power of drug cartels, mafias, and private security agencies. Instead of borders, there would be moving "centers" of power, as in the Middle Ages. Many of these layers would be in motion. Replacing fixed and abrupt lines on a flat space would be a shifting pattern of buffer entities.... Henceforward the map of the world will never be static. This future map—in a sense, the "Last Map"—will be an ever-mutating representation of chaos. (75)

This is the best description I've come across of the Ashberian tradition, with the caveat that Ashbery's work, if not that of the more politically-minded Language Poets who are sometimes linked to him, is less overtly concerned with power and control, and thus his vision is perhaps less fearful of the future than what we find in Kaplan.

In a poem from *The Double Dream of Spring*, "Evening in the Country"—read both "countryside" and "country as state"—we are timid witnesses ("cautious yet free/ On the edge") to last displays of power, "the unblinking chariot" rolling "Into the vast open, the incredible violence and yielding/ Turmoil that is to be our route." The sun gets largest just before it goes under; we can but watch the grand, horrible show. Ashbery describes the sunset as "ten thousand helmeted footsoldiers,/ A Spanish armada stretching to the horizon, all/ Absolutely motionless until the hour to strike"—but, as we know, ultimately fail in the case of the armada.

In Ashbery we have, to a significant degree beyond Lowell, "an ever-mutating representation of chaos," and, paradoxically, Ashbery finds his truest voice in just this chaos. Vernon Shetley distinguishes between New Critical poetics and Ashbery's Postmodernism:

> The New Critics delighted in teasing out ambiguities, but saw those ambiguities as building to form coherent, if paradoxical, structures; their notion was ultimately spacial. Ashbery's syntactical puzzles, however, arise in the form of sentences that seem to change their projected shape in mid-stream.... Ashbery's ambiquities are fluid rather than structures...."
> (119)

In general his poems do not proceed in stages, that is, dialectically, but by mutation and accretion. Ashbery creates a multidimensional space–discrete yet related contexts, the whole of which is everchanging into new contexts. Paradoxically, Lowell's dialectical, multitemporal approach leads to stasis, whereas Ashbery's nondialectical, multispacial approach is a vehicle for movement: the self is never at rest; it circulates among its properties. For Lowell, everything is outside; for Ashbery, nothing is outside. Thus Lowell, the confessionalist, writes from the outside in; while Ashbery, the hermeticist, writes from the inside out.

"Self-Portrait in A Convex Mirror" introduces early on the complications inherent in the self-language matrix Ashbery's work tends to inhabit (as we, contemporary readers, tend to inhabit). Parmigianino, the sixteenth-century mannerist painter, set himself "'With great art to copy all that he saw in the glass,'" Ashbery writes quoting Vasari, then adds, "Chiefly his reflection, of which the portrait/ Is the reflection once removed." The portrait is a microcosm, a miniature version of what the artist saw, "life englobed," himself displayed. The soul of the artist, which "establishes itself," is really "not a soul,/ has no secret, is small, and it fits/ Its hollow perfectly: its room, our moment of attention." We readers of Ashbery's poem are twice removed, yet we are necessary spectators. Without "our moment of attention," however hollow, Ashbery's wandering soul could not establish itself, in the small hollow we've saved for it (although our attentions also rob the portrait of its soul, its subjectivity, its freedom).

Parmigianino's self portrait is an object in a world of objects *and* it reflects, by virtue of its convexity, all the world, that is, all the world the artist saw, "which was enough for his purpose." The whole, the Big Picture, so to speak, turns out to be just a picture of one's self, a self-portrait. So Parmigianino's self-portrait is comprehensive, complete, contains self and world, and yet it is just one object, one version of things, "a whisper out of time," as the last line of the poem says. Part of the painting's beauty derives from its position in the reflecting light of Ashbery's and our own wistful sense of time and history: "But it is certain that/ What is beautiful seems so only in relation to a specific/ Life, experienced or not, channeled into some form/ Steeped in the nostalgia of a collective past." Here Ashbery approaches an idea of the past which is not far from Lowell's–Lowell finding a similar idea in the work of Dutch masters. If Ashbery is less angst-driven than Lowell, he is yet romantic; indeed he is much more the transcendentalist than Lowell, whose New England heritage in his case pushes him more toward the metaphysical (as it did T.S Eliot) and expressionistic. Ashbery's characteristic disclaimers–"experienced or not"–and ambivalent responses–"channeled" as completion or restriction?–provide for even as they complicate his romanticism. Shetley writes, "Certainly, the poet of linguistic free-play exists in Ashbery, but exists in combination with, and in some sense permits the existence of, the Keatsian lyricist. Ashbery himself says that "'all my stuff is romantic poetry, rather than metaphysical or surrealist'" (132).

From what we learn of Ashbery from his other poems, and from his art criticism, it is not surprising that he would respond so strongly–if ambivently–to Parmigianino's painting. The painting is personal and planetary, intimate and large; Ashbery, like other contemporary writers with a post-historical bent, tends to cut out the moral/historical ground of familial, social, and political structures, which so occupies Lowell. There is no great Other in Ashbery, no History in the large sense; indeed Otherness and History are objectified and reduced by and in objects-- which are, in some sense, one's self.

The collapsing of time and self which becomes more prominent as Lowell's poetic career proceeds is a kind of starting point for Ashbery; for him, the simulacra–the reduction of the world to reflective objects, the siphoning off of desire as a result of its implication in institutional and commodified space–is a given. Whereas one may regret this state of affairs, feeling that one has been forced to "try to begin living in what/ Has now become a slum," the modest upside is that heroic dreams of the self are dismantled so that "Something like living occurs, a movement/ Out of the dream into its codification." In a review of "The New Realists" exhibition catalogue, 1962, Ashbery writes:

> The unmanageable vastness of our experience, the regrettable unpredictability of our aims and tastes, have been seized on by the New Realists as the core of a continuing situation; that of man on one side and a colorful indifferent universe on the other. There is no moral to be drawn from this, and in any case the artist's work on this as on other occasions is not preaching or even mediation, but translation and exegesis, in order to show us where the balance of power lies in the yet-once-again altered scheme of things. Today it seems to repose in the objects that surround us; that is our perceptions of them or, simply and once again, in ourselves. (83)[5]

We cannot look beyond ourselves, both Lowell and Ashbery seem to say; this Kierkegardian dictum is pervasive in contemporary poetry. However, Ashbery is more "personal" than Lowell, especially in Ashbery's willingness to allow intimate and often domestic gestures of everyday life, as well as everyday "things," a central place in his work. He is also more cosmic: Ashbery maintains, often with a melancholic overtone, a Zen Buddhist-like acceptance of the world's indifferent, evermutating yet essentially unified nature. "Changes are merely/

Features of the whole." Out of this personal-cosmic orientation Ashbery gains a measure of freedom, for both good and ill, from the familial, social, and historical forces which tend to circumscribe Lowell's sense of selfhood. But more importantly, Ashbery's orientation causes him to appraise Parmigianino's portrait as being but one (beautiful and thought-provoking) arrangement, in time and space, in a multiplicity and continuum of self-world arrangements, all of which, as in 3D computer modeling, may or may not exist in the physical world and exist only in schematic/ mathematical form. The world is not "finished" in any sense of the word. Indeed, ultimately Ashbery appears to reject the fine completeness of Parmiginino's painting--"this flow like an hourglass/ Without varying in climate or quality"–its desire, and presumably Ashbery's own, in the past, to ape naturalness, which "may be a first step/ Toward achieving an inner calm/ But it is the first step only, and often/ Remains a frozen gesture of welcome etched/ On the air materializing behind it,/ A convention." An "exotic/ Refuge within an exhausted world" is no longer acceptable, though "Once it seemed so perfect–glass on the fine/ Freckled skin, lips moistened as though about to part/ Releasing speech, and the familiar look/ Of clothes and furniture that one forgets."

The self-portrait is, as mentioned earlier, "a whisper out of time"– a message from a different time period and a message that exists outside of time. But looking at it we not only visit Parmiginino's world but feel the urge to move beyond and outside of it: "Each person/ Has one big theory to explain the universe/ But it doesn't tell the whole story/ And in the end it is what is outside him/ That matters, to him and especially to us...." The role of the artist is to create a mirror reflection of his or her *own* individual self and world–or as Stevens writes in "The Planet on the Table": "His self and the sun were one/ And his poems, although makings of his self,/ Were no less makings of the sun." Making the sun–creating a model universe–occupies Ashbery. Only in this way can the artist move beyond and outside of not only his predecessors but also his own "big theory." David

Bergman is right when he argues that Ashbery's solution is to "advocate that artists take up separate and individual spiritual pilgrimages to find their personal visions" (xv). Each artist's vision will be distinct, private, that is, strange, and thus not merely human. In an essay on Parmigianino, Ashbery opens with a quote from Giorgio De Chirico that he goes on to associate with the appeal of Parmigianino's work:

> It must not be forgotten that a picture must always testify to a profound sensation, and that profound means strange, and that strange means little-known or completely unknown. For a work of art to be truly immortal, it must completely transcend human limitations. In this way it will approach dreams and the spirit of childhood. (*Reported Sightings* 31)

Ashbery miniaturizes and privatizes History, incorporates it, makes it his own, available, first come, first serve, to everyone. There is a whispering, ghostly, childlike intimacy, similar to in Whitman--and like Whitman, economies of immediate exchange. As he says in "Song of Myself":

> What is commonest, cheapest, nearest, easiest, is Me. Me going in for my chances, spending for vast returns, Adorning myself to bestow myself on the first that will take me, Not asking the sky to come down to my good will, Scattering it freely forever.

The Future of the Poetry of Consciousness

But unlike Whitman–especially late Whitman–Ashbery eschews direct comment on public issues. Harold Bloom writes, "It is fascinating though sad to see Ashbery omitting from his recent *Selected Poems* so many of the poems one loves best: 'Evening in the Country,' 'Fragment,' 'The One Thing That Can Save America' among them. Evidently he does not regard them as original enough, or perhaps they are exquisitely painful to him" (x). I'm puzzled myself by the omission of "Evening in the Country" and "The One Thing That Can Save America," but I would hazard a guess that after a while Ashbery found their more overt political content and their references to America uncomfortable. One might also imagine that part of their appeal for Bloom lies in just this more specific Americanness. I, too, find a great deal to admire in those two poems, and I've no doubt that part of what draws me to them is that they take place closer to "home" than most other Ashbery poems. Ashbery's basic instincts, his dispersion of subjectivity and his focus on things (if not entirely Williams's "the thing itself"), are very American: indeed in combination these two instincts *simplify* the world. Since consciousness is unknowable in any absolute sense, and is everchanging, one does best to pay attention to moments and to immediate objects. And one does best to avoid large claims. Ashbery appears to feel, as compared to Lowell and others who take a more dialectical approach--who think we will become something other and better–that only by indirection or really lack of direction, only by not memorializing what we see before us at any particular moment do we remain available to what rounds the corner, which cannot be predicted. And yet, to my mind we also live by traditions, by customs–in a specific country, county, city, family, etc.–and of these Ashbery speaks little.

To enter into one of his poems is to enter original and mind-expanding territory; it is to lose one's sense of balance and thus understand the strange and impalpable nature of consciousness, in ways similar to the following lines from Whitman's "Crossing Brooklyn Ferry": "The impalpable sustenance of me from all things at all hours of the day,/ The simple, compact, well-joined scheme, myself disintegrated, every one disintegrated yet part of the scheme...." But I'm not sure what to *do* with an Ashbery poem, how to apply a journey into Ashbery's world to my world, except perhaps to ease up and accept things as they come to me–and read another Ashbery poem! The self-referential nature of his poetic world causes me to feel, at least in part, that his poems exist, like Parmigianino's self-portrait, outside of time and space, too far beyond "human limitations." Yet

Douglas Crase's more positive reading of Ashbery's apparent hermeticism also strikes me as true:

> The difficulty with Ashbery is that is poetry is *so* public, so accurately a picture of the world we live in, that it scarcely resembles anything we have ever known. Just so, the present is indeed a world none of us has ever known, because the words to describe it can be put together only after the fact. When the poet does put them together the combination comes as a shock. Understandably, one may at first regard that combination as hermetically private. Only gradually do we realize that it describes the public world we were living in just moments ago–that some prophet has arrived with news of the commonwealth. (127)

Lowell, of course, can seem at times all-too-human, or perhaps too Lowell. But a charged sense of human struggle, in historical context, is palpable in Lowell and reminds us, I believe, of the power poetry has to engage the world. Furthermore, Lowell's later poetry, in particular, adds an important voice to the American tradition of a poetry of consciousness. Yet we have taken the poetry of consciousness–a poetry of dreamlike abstraction, simultaneity, and multiplicity, to define it further–about as far as it can profitably go; some form of relocation in a specific geographical and ethical climate as well as a renewed attention to the various formal properties of verse, could perhaps bring back a weighty richness of language, form, and felt-life seldom found since Lowell. To wish for a poet to be somewhat other than he or she is–to wish, for instance, that Emily Dickinson got out of the house more often–is foolish. Poets have a better sense of what they can and can not do, and of how they must live in order to get their work done, than we do. Furthermore, Lowell and Ashbery strike me as the strongest American poets of recent years. Lowell's last book, *Day by Day*, is remarkable, nearly on a par with *Life Studies* and *For the Union Dead*; Ashbery remains a poet of striking felicity and ingenuity–often precisely by "carefully" leaving out "descriptions of pain, and sex, and how shiftily/ people behave toward each other" as he writes in a recent poem, "The Problem of Anxiety." But if one *were* wishing, one might hope for an American poet with both the city-state and the American grain scope of a Whitman, or at least a William Carlos Williams, for a poet who is as much a son (and daughter, father, mother, brother, sister, comrade) of some locale as he is of universal consciousness, and of some regional dialect as he is of the International Style, and of America as he is of borderlands.

4

TRAVELING THROUGH THE DARK: WILLIAM STAFFORD AND THE SURREALISM OF THE FAR WEST

"In a world this big almost anything can happen, or almost happen, exploring upward, beyond. Finally you know this."

—William Stafford, "Ashbery"

As an outgrowth of the Sixties and in response to the influx of people and translations from all corners of the world, a particular kind of neoromantic literature became prominent: the surreal. Some form of surrealist literature has found a home in all regions of the country, including such historically-minded and surrealist-resistant areas as New England and the South. Lowell, for one, is increasingly surrealist from *Life Studies* (1959) onward. Yet an American surrealism, or, more accurately, "near surrealism," has primarily been developed in the West, where the stark juxtaposition of nature and machine as well as the juxtapositions of a wide range of subcultures creates an art of dreamlike displacement.

The spectacular and desolate curve of sky and land, of mountain and plain, and of high plains and desert has long contributed to making western American literature somewhat more otherworldly than the literatures of the eastern, central, and southern United States. Western American literature is derived from the sun and moon as much as it is from the earth and society: the cosmic or metaphysical dimension is strong, and a rootless, solitary, and reticent attitude prevails. The recent massive growth of the western U.S. had led to a confrontation between frontier attitudes and the necessities of a highly complex technological and multicultural society. This conflict encourages a derealization in the way the world is experienced and described, even in a writer such as William Stafford, who, as Robert Bly writes, "looks to the palpable and hearable" (x).

Poets as unlike as Stafford and Gregory Corso, whom I use here as parameters of Sixties poetry styles in the West, inherit and develop a new geography. A brief listing of some of the West's more interesting contemporary poets—Theodore Roethke, Kenneth Rexroth, Robert Duncan, Charles Bukowski, Thom Gunn, John Haines, Norman Dubie, Joy Harjo—indicates the importance of the near-surrealist/neoromantic strain. There is a strong sense of the "wild" in all of these poets, and a strong sense of the significance of "wilderness" in most of them. Richard Hugo is here discussed, along with Stafford and Corso, at some length, and serves as a kind of dark intermediary between them.

In the end, projecting beyond the Sixties, I argue that Stafford is the poet of wilderness surrealism most identifiable as thoroughly in the American grain, by virtue of his continuing faith in the open road, and his sense of being "at home" no matter where he is. In Stafford, outsiderness receives a new twist: there is no such thing as a permanent home and yet we are never disconnected nor displaced. This is a distinctly postmodern attitude and links Stafford to the future in ways unavailable to either Beat or Deep Image poets. Stafford's postmodernism belies Charles Altieri's notion that Stafford is a poet trapped in the scenic mode of contemporary poetry in which a "reticent, plain-speaking, and self-reflective speaker within a narratively presented scene" evokes "a sense of loss" (10).

Gregory Corso: Beat Surrealist

Many of the urban surrealists of the late Fifties and early Sixties, who had gathered in New York, found it necessary and profitable to shift the focus of their concerns to the "Wild West," finding a center of activity in San Francisco. Although some such as John Ashbery and Frank O'Hara stayed home (while also venturing to Paris), others, especially those associated with the Beat movement, headed west. In *The Dharma Bums*, Jack Kerouac describes what they found:

> It took exactly the entire twenty-five miles to get out of the smog of Los Angeles, the sun was clear in Riverside. I exulted to see a beautiful dry riverbottom with white sand and just a trickle river in the middle as we rolled over the bridge into Riverside. I was looking for my first chance to camp out for the night and try out my new ideas. But at the hot bus station a Negro saw me with my pack and came over and said he was part Mohawk and when I told him I was going back up the road to sleep in that riverbottom he said "No sir, you can't do that, cops in this town are the toughest in the state...."
>
> This ain't no India, is it," I said, sore, and walked off anyway to try it. ... I laughed thinking what would happen if I was Fuke the Chinese sage of the ninth century who wandered around China constantly ringing his bell. The only alternative to sleeping out, hopping freights, and doing what I wanted, I saw in vision would be to just sit with a hundred other patients in front of a nice television set in a madhouse, where we could be "supervised." ... I saw many cop cruising cars and they were looking for me suspiciously: sleek, well-paid cops in brand-new cars with all that expensive radio equipment to see that no bhikku slept in his grove tonight. (95-96)

Essential characteristics of the Beat surreal are revealed in this passage. Surrealism, generally defined, is the juxtaposition of elements from different space-times. Here Kerouac interfaces the open landscape of the vast west with efficient, and malevolent, machines of the new world. We also have references to several cultures, ancient and modern. The traditional American images of the "machine in the garden" and the "melting pot" are incorporated, but the emphasis in on the fear and loathing they represent and produce on the last frontier. Kerouac's swift moving style enhances the effect of all these elements, here juxtaposed, passing before one's eyes as though part of a strange, unholy, dream. And finally, Kerouac's odd yet touching sense of humor–the Negro claiming that he is part Mohawk, the narrator's desire to try out his new ideas–gives the scene, however unholy, the feeling of surprising, wide-eyed joy that only the deepest melancholy can generate. Like other surrealists, Kerouac has decided to "dig" rather than lament the strange and lonesome world he has come across.

The myth of the Beat hero is well described by Dorothy Van Ghent. Both Corso and Allen Ginsburg refer to ancient cultures in the last line of their respective poems, "Marriage" and "A Supermarket in California," indicating, perhaps, what Van Ghent calls the "authentic archaic lines" (213) of the Beat myth. Yet the Beat myth has tended to obscure significant differences among Beat poets. Ginsberg works out of a tradition of exhortation and lament, Bibilical in its orientation (despite the inversions of traditional good and evil), while Corso often becomes more of a clown than a seer, and tends toward an "objective" presentation of the bare metaphysical facts that, more often than not, overwhelm man, Buster Keaton fashion.

Corso, much like his fellow New Yorker O'Hara, explores an urban wilderness, concentrating on social organization. Yet Corso's move to San Francisco signifies an important difference between the two poets. Corso, as is the case with other Beats, is usually in flight from something. Whereas O'Hara, in postmodern fashion, is more accepting of modern city life–and indeed delights in it–Corso remains more of an outsider. O'Hara, in *Selected Poems*, asks in his laconic and domestic manner, "Oh Jane, is there no more frontier?" (25), while

Corso, an apocalyptic comedian, states his misgivings more forcibly, in a poem from *Mindfield*,

> I am a great American
> I am almost nationalistic about it!
> I love America like a madness!
> But I am afraid to return to America
> I'm even afraid to go into the American Express—

Corso does not embrace nature, or sees nature as not embracing its local products. In a poem written in memory of Kerouac, "Elegiac Feelings American," Kerouac is portrayed as truly American yet someone who stands nonetheless "upon America like a rootless flat-bottomed tree." Even direct description of nature turns Baudelarian in Corso's hands: in "Sunset, he writes,

> Falls the sun
>   slowly
>   like
>   a
>   shot circle

Richard Hugo: Deep Image Surrealist

Richard Hugo, a native Westerner, has perhaps gone the furthest in terms of emphasizing the lonesome quality of the West, especially his own Northwest. This lonesomeness is a product of, and ever leads to, remote places. Gary Snyder, often labeled a "Beat" as well as a nature poet, serves as a vehicle for showing some of connections and differences between Corso and Hugo. In Snyder's poetry an attention to the natural order of the universe produces a contemplative approach to the world and leads, ultimately, to a reticence which has an effect quite similar to Corso's urban wildness. Although Corso employs a far wider range of tones than Snyder (who is more transcendentalist than surrealist), both poets usually suppress the links in the chain, that is, connecting and explanatory matter. The things themselves are permitted to speak for themselves, which creates (at least the impression of) a more objective presentation, beyond personal anguish and lamentation. O'Hara was the first to point out the central "brevity" of Corso's work (*Standing Still* 83). However, in Snyder as in Hugo, the world is not so much the lunatic world Corso describes as it is a kind of ancient, pastoral dream world. Snyder's reticence–his unwillingness to level too much blame, his acceptance of the rule of nature, his willingness to let the old gods speak to our time–is in keeping with the code of mystics and poets of both Asia and the United States.

In "Stafford Country" Hugo points to an element of reticence in the American–especially western American–tradition: "Where land is flat, words are far apart./ Each word is seen coming from far off,/ a calm storm, almost familiar, across/ the plain. The word floats by, alive." This is indeed Stafford country; Hugo's landscape however is farther north, less open, darker, nearer to the sea. It is peopled by derelicts, seafarers, Indians, and common laborers, all who move, often courageously, within the ruins of their lives. Hugo is the Northwest's Russian poet, battling forces of the early dark and melancholy, though believing, finally, in the possibilities of dignity and transformation. Hugo's strong identification with the many-voiced world of common life produces a kind of ventriloquism, with Hugo speaking *for* the lost. In his poems one life leads, like a river, toward other waters; one word merges with another. Hugo seeks to subsume, within himself, the rise and fall and rise again of lives caught in the waves of a certain place and time. And these lives can do little more than talk about what has happened to them, or didn't happen, as in "Port Townsend":

A novel fakes a start in every bar,
gives way to gin and talk. The talk gives way
to memories of elk, and elk was never here.
Freighters never give this town a second look.
The dead are buried as an afterthought

and when the tide comes glittering with smelt
the grebes have gone to look for meaty ports.

Strangeness and unreality is central to Hugo's poetry, as if we we only passing through toward some unknown other side.

This unknown other side had been labeled, in our time, the "unconscious." In a discussion of the surrealist element in James Wright's poetry, James E.B. Breslin writes: "Wright does not present the clean, hard-edge perception of physical surface that we get in much of imagism; instead, his images, carrying suggestions of invisible, magical realities beyond the literal world, seem to float up out of the unconscious at the moment when the boundaries between self and world are crossed. They are *deep* images" (194).

Like Wright, Hugo often fuses two disparate words or images, drawing from the unconscious a marriage of self and world. "The Blond Road" illustrates how Hugo's impressionistic and melancholy images and tones animate landscapes, until the landscape itself begins to speak for him. Hugo's ventriloquism is not only a product of the multiple personalities of the self, often released by the dark and drink, it is also an outgrowth of the multiple non- human presences of the self, often released when traveling alone on an "empty" road.

This road dips and climbs but never bends.
The line it finally is strings far beyond
my sight, still the color of useless dirt.
Trees are a hundred greens in varying light
as sky breaks black on silver over and in
the sea. No one home or car. No shacks
abandoned to the storm. On one side, miles
of high grass; on the other, weather
and the sea reflecing tons of a wild day.

In the following stanza Hugo makes a deft transition from "wild day" to "The wind is from Malay," but it is the sentence which follows that which really causes the twist or torque in our apprehension of the scene: "Tigers in the wind/ makes lovers claw each other orange." From this point on the poem is inhabited by many varieties of "wildlife"; there is a strange merging, a synergy of the great chain of being–although angels remain just outside the frame. Or they do until, perhaps, the last line of the poem, when "stone birds" go "climbing to their names" (in a dream unrealizable). Again I find Brelin's comments applicable: "It is this distance between the two terms of his metaphors that has prompted many critics to describe Wright as surrealist; yet this label disguises the crucial fact that Wright's images (like Bly's) embody a vision that is closer to that of Walt Whitman than that of Andre Breton" (181). Breslin finds a Whitmanesque natural harmony in Wright's use of images.

Hugo lacks the light/dark airiness and quickness of James Wright. Hugo imbues the deep image tradition with history and accumulating detail in a manner similar to Lowell's "The Quacker Graveyard in Nantucket" and "Skunk Hour." There is a leap of joy and lyrical transmutation in the last line of "The Blond Road"- both dear to surrealism–but finally there is throughout an underlying grotesquery and sadness, which perhaps evokes a world more Naturalistic than harmonious. Rarely are crises in Hugo enlivened by a Kerouac-like humor, wild and joyful, digging the world. Hugo's sardonic humor grows out of the black tangle of the twarted lives and ruined landscape that held him in thrall–often to the point of confessional-like despair. In "The Art of Poetry," he writes,

> And think,
> sad Raymond, of the wrong way maturation came.
> Wanting only those women you despised, imitating the
> voice of every man you envied. The slow walk home
> alone. Pause at the door. The screaming kitchen. And
> every day this window, loathing the real horizon.

William Stafford: Surrealist in the American Grain

William Stafford hails from Kansas. His poems employ a flatter, more common, clean- eyed diction than anyone mentioned so far: the Midwest is the language of prose. Yet Stafford's poems often display surrealist tendencies–his inclination for deep images and reticence transmuting common-voice materials.

Midwest poets, especially of the so-called Iowa School, resist oratorical flourishes, preferring deep images to exclamations, cries, chants, etc. With Stafford we have traveled a long way from the performance tendencies of Corso. But in Stafford's work a gentle, quiet near- surrealism emerges, derived from the earth and common life, although it is often confrontations with urban life which provoke the surrealist response. Stafford's work is akin to that of Stephen Crane, who is perhaps the first surrealist in the American grain. John Berryman writes of Crane: "His work is wrung as clear [of the "documentary burden"] as Poe's or Hawthorne's; and unlike theirs his revolt did not drive him into fantasy or allegory. His eyes remained open on the world" (4). Stafford, like Corso, keeps his eyes on the "real" world, but he appears to also believe that realism is not equipped (or no longer equipped) to describe its affective colors and structures.

In Stafford's *Traveling through the Dark* we can see this. The book reveals a clean yet impressionistic style we associate with Midwesterners like Hemingway, Cather, and Weldon Kees, but at times the poems also verge on surrealism. In the famous title poem, for instance, a doe, carrying her unborn fawn, is found dead on the edge of a narrow road by a driver of a car.

His headlights provide the only illumination, white and red, in the darkness; and the only sound is the "purr" of the "steady engine." It is a frozen, nearly silent scene–"she had stiffened already, almost cold"–although the doe is also warm because "her fawn lay waiting/ alive, still, never to be born." The most audible presences in the poem are the ruminations of the speaker and the wilderness itself, which "listens" (the steady five-beat line which runs through most of the poem contributes to the sense that the wilderness is alive–pulsing).

The speaker concludes the poem: "I thought hard for all–my only swerving–,/ then pushed her over the edge into the river." The word "swerve," repeated in the poem (in two forms), is central to the way a Stafford poem moves, that is, by swerving away from a clearly seen object (the deer in the road) toward the apprehension of that object in the curve of space and light, as well as in one's own thoughts ("I stood in the glare of the warm exhaust turning red;"), until we once more see the object in relation to its swirling environment, and often, moving within the stream of the place's consciousness. The activity of the poem–the movement of the speaker's mind through the dark– can be seen in the tonal shifts of the successive stanzas, four quatrains and a closing two-line verse unit. The first of these five stanzas details, in a matter of fact manner, the stark picture of the dead deer and speaker's thought that it "is usually best to roll them into the canyon." After dragging the doe off the road–stanza two ends with the detail that she "was large in the belly"–we discover in stanza three, as the speaker touches the side of the doe, that there is yet-to-be-born life within death. So the mood of the poem is gently yet radically altered, as one's responsibility to human life–other cars that will be traveling through the dark–is coupled with one's responsibility to the unborn, "never to be born." The stanza ends: "Beside that mountain I hesitated."

In stanza four we have the juxtaposition of machine and wilderness, complicated by the animal "purr" of the motor and the human listening of the wilderness. In the final two-lines stanza the speaker's thoughts "for us all," which is a kind of false "swerving" away from necessity as well as one's own solitariness, are dissolved in action, the doe and her fawn "pushed...over the edge into the river." This river of thought and action is, of course, the river of life and death, but more importantly it is the river of the poem itself, its process.

The impressionistic rendering of light and of movement with stasis in "Traveling through the Dark" nicely dovetails into the opening lines of the book's second poem, "In Medias Res": "On Main one night when they sounded the chimes/ my father was

ahead in shadow, my son/ behind coming into the streetlight...."
The urban and historical details of this second poem, and their
power to alter and distort vision, as well as the simple juxtaposition
of the two poems, increases the sense that we are in a world more
surreal than realistic or impressionistic. In the beginning of the
poem we find ourselves in the midst of a family history, a "one-
stride God." The chimes of death and heaven have sounded for the
speaker's father and will sound for them all. A synesthesia of sound
and light creates an otherworldly atmosphere; and each new line
blends another family figure (or figures) into the celestial scene.
At the end of the first stanza they are "all walkers in a cloud." But
a significant shift in tone and imagery occurs in the second stanza,
one that remakes the poem as a whole into a kaleidoscopic vision
of betrayal:

> I saw pictures, windows taking shoppers
> where the city went, a great shield hammering out,
> my wife loving the stations on that shield
> and following into the shades calling back.
> I had not thought to know the hero quite so well.
> "Aeneas," I cried, "just man, defender!"
> And our town burned and burned.

In the brilliant image of the (store?) windows we have, once again,
the characteristic surrealistic movement from impressionistic blend-
ing to leaping, curving, superimposed images which destroy individual compositions in favor of fiery juxtapositions of distantly related
space-times and distantly related peoples. The "town" burns and
burns in the light cast by the city. The contrast of natural town life
and unnatural city life, a version of the conflict between open landscape and machine, is made clear (though rather indirectly).

However, in this poem we have little sense of Beat joy, noticeable
in Kerouac, Corso, and to some degree in Snyder, or even the deli-
cious northern melancholy of Roethke and Hugo.

Stafford's is a quieter, more even-handed approach, and Charles Altieri, in *Self and sensibility*, commenting on Stafford's early poem "Ceremony," is right when he warns of the limitations of such a modest and, for Altieri, controlled style:

> Naturalness in Stafford is so elaborately controlled, one wonders how any feelings not certified as "poetic" can flow on or how any humble self can swim such a river. The poem itself utterly lacks fluidity because we are never allowed to forget how each detail must perform the symbolic chore of preparing for the "surprising" visionary consummation. (3)

But even as far back as *Traveling through the Dark* and certainly after that time, Stafford's imagistic wit provides grounds for what Judith Kitchen, in response to Altieri, describes as Stafford's "intuitive sense of the rift between reality and language"(33). Stafford himself writes: "I feel a lot more harmony with someone like John Ashbery and his assumptions about poetry...than I do with many other poets... those people that seem to feel that think they are corraling ultimate truth.... I think poetry is ultimately playful, no matter what anyone says. And Ashbery is explicit about this" (qtd. in Stitt 179). Stafford rarely calls attention to the rift between reality and language, or truth and language, in a manner that might satisfy the dialectically-minded Altieri, but it is difficult to read Stafford very long without an awareness of slippage in both language and the poet's persona. The deep-image heritage of image and revelation is given the slip by this singularly elusive poet precisely because he, unlike Corso or Hugo, but like Whitman, is everywhere the same. At home everywhere (and yes, perhaps nowhere).

The third poem in *Traveling through the Dark*, "Elegy," opens with a witty, metaphysical, and mildly ironic image of common life: "The responsible sound of the lawnmower/ puts a net under the afternoon." One might call this a surrealist image, but Stafford's repartee is often so gentle it has the effect of softening and undercutting the surrealist edge–yet this is just what frees up the poem from any sort of controlled, mannered, or heavily political tone (which *does* mar, as Altieri point out in *Enlarging the Temple,* some of Robert Bly's deep image work). Dislocation is neither unexpected nor memorialized in Stafford. He does not turn any certain place into an object-fetish, as (too oversimplify) O'Hara makes of New York, or Corso makes of the Beat World, or Hugo makes of lonely places.[1] Nothing is particularly exotic to Stafford; all is part of an extended network.

"Elegy" continues the surrealistic, oneiric movement of the book as a whole:

> Remember in the Southwest going down the canyons?
> We turned off the engine, the tires went hoarse
> picking up sound out of turned away mountains;
> We felt the secret sky lean down.

The landscape of the west imbues this surrealism with something that goes beyond, I believe, traditional, and rather passive, appeals to the unconscious, or to the lyrical, or to some sort of dissociation of sensibility–or some "immanentist" revelation, which Altieri discounts as ahistorical. Landscape provides for the possibility of action in the objective world. The curving sounds and sights of the poem give us the feeling (best known from Westerns) that most anything could happen here, including revelation–"At the sight of angels or anything unusual/ you are to mark the spot with a cross..." (although the "anything unusual" provides the characteristic Stafford disclaimer). Furthermore, the tableau of machine and landscape reminds us that, however static and scenic the description, new conjunctions of time and space have taken place. There is still an open road, and no matter what happens, or doesn't happen, Stafford is ready, and at home, living in the present. He writes in a late poem, "The Dream of Now," from *Passwords*:

When you wake to the dream of now
from night and its other dream,
you carry day out of the dark
like a flame.

When spring comes north, and flowers
unfold from earth and its even sleep,
you lift summer on your breath
lest it be lost ever so deep.

Your life you live by the light you find
and follow it on as well as you can,
carrying through the darkness whereever you go
your one little fire that will start again.

Stafford is one of the representative poets of the Information Age despite his being a product of the Depression and the late Industrial Age; and no doubt the ahistorical nature of the Information Age will inevitably leave a critic such as Altieri (and myself, for that matter) somewhat disappointed in the poetry of our time. Here it is perhaps enough to say that wilderness surrealism, especially as handled by Stafford, provides ground for reorienting modern consciousness toward a connectedness between all peoples and places, and toward a poetics that is not so much personal as planetary.

5

MEN, MENACE, AND TRANSCENDENCE IN RAYMOND CARVER

Raymond Carver's epistemology derives from common physical and social activities. My first sight of Carver happened to be seeing him and Tess Gallagher, his girlfriend and future wife, emerge together–laughing–from the UC Santa Cruz coed bathroom, in the dorm where we fellow writing conferees were staying. It was 1978. Carver had one-year of sobriety, was newly separated, and had just published his first major story collection, *Will You Please Be Quiet, Please?* I recognized him from the dust jacket of his book. I also recognized immediately that they were laughing at having shared a coed bathroom, on that most liberal of college campuses. But the bathroom incident, memorable in itself, has acquired an additional, random, and serendipitous meaning for me since then as a result of something I've come to notice in Carver's stories: bathroom references.[1] The repeated if often hidden bathroom allusions (bordering at times on the potty talk of little boys) serve an important function in those stories: we are ever reminded of the power of necessity, of elemental existence, whether excretory, sexual, medical, or broadly practical. His method is experiential and empirical. We are always "going," to use a key Carver word, Carver as "participle-loving" as Ezra Greenspan (expanding on an insight of Randall Jarrell's) has written of Walt Whitman being (92) , and as characteristically American, I would argue. American Male, in particular. As is the case for Ernest Hemingway, the short story provides Carver with a form suited to a brusque, mythic American masculinity. Speculative, mythic questioning and transcendental connections (however rare, in the case of the latter) are products in Carver of intensive drinking and eating; social–primarily male homosocial–activities; and aggressive talk–all, generally, fostering and taking place in the context of violent remaking of one sort or another. Perhaps only in the late story "Cathedral" is an accommodation made between masculine frontier instincts and domestic social convention.

"Which way is this going?"

In an interview in *The Paris Review*, Carver describes the end of his drinking days: "The last year of my drinking, 1977, I was in a recovery center twice, as well as one hospital; and I spent a few days in a place called DeWitt near San Jose, California. DeWitt used to be, appropriately enough, a hospital for the criminally insane" (316). Carver's drinking history finds representation in almost all of his stories. Often times the drinking motif is part and parcel with, not surprisingly, going to the bathroom. In "Why Don't You Dance?", the first story from his second major collection, *What We Talk About When We Talk About Love*, the boy is drinking and says, of drink, "'It goes to your head... I'm getting it in the head'" (8). As in this cited instance, sexual innuendo–in this case, getting head–is also often part of the equation. The question of how to deal with women is central. There's a masculine and violent cast to the stories. In the collection's title story, two couples sit around a table drinking gin. Mel, a heart surgeon, discourses on love, becoming more and more confounded the more he drinks and the more he attempts to pin down and restrict the definition of love: "'There was a time when I thought I loved my first wife more than life itself. But now I hate her guts. I do. How do you explain that? What happened to that love? What happened to it, is what I'd like to know'" (144). Carver suggests that one often has little idea which way things–conversations, relationships, etc.–are likely to go. In "Cathedral," the title story of his third major collection, a husband, wife, and her friend–"the blind man"–pass a roach: "My wife sat on the sofa between the blind man and me. I passed her the number. She took it and toked and then passed it back to me. 'Which way is this going?' she said" (367), which we might take to reference not just the roach, but also their evening together.

Violent accidents–a car accident in both"What We Talk About When We Talk About Love" and "The Bath" (from the same collection), for example–are regular elements (Carver worked in hospitals as a young man). Life can easily flow out of us–water a particularly common part of the overlapping motifs involving "going." In "So Much Water So Close to Home," a woman is found dead floating in a stream by four fishermen, four buddies, who are off on a weekend trip away from their wives. The death remains unexplained, although here it is clearly not an accident as the woman is young, attractive, and naked. The men are not sure what they should do about the body and whether they should immediately report the find. They are several miles from town: "They pleaded fatigue, the late hour, the fact that the girl wasn't going anywhere" (81). They even wash their cooking and eating "things" (81) in the river where the girl is. In the movie *Short Cuts*, drawn from Carver stories and poems, director Robert Altman has one of the men piss in the water where the naked girl floats. In fact, this man discovers the girl while he is pissing. At one point in the short story, the wife of one of the men, and the story's narrator, is driving alone down a back road–she's distraught over her husband's failure to interrupt his fishing trip to report the girl's death–when a man driving behind her "goes past" (81). She pulls off the side of the road and soon hears his pickup coming back. She locks her doors and rolls up the windows, but he gets out of his truck and taps on the glass. The scene continues:

"Is everything all right in there? How come you're so locked up?"

I shake my head.

"Roll down your window." He shakes his head and looks at the highway and then at the highway and then back at me. "Roll it down now."

"Please," I say, "I have to go." (86)

The first line above could be taken as someone outside a bathroom stall concerned about someone inside who is constipated–"locked up." And it's hard not to notice the male anatomical innuendo of "I shake my head" and "He shakes his head." Indeed the narrator seems to momentarily consider the man's apparent sexual come on. Sex and violence lurk on the back roads of America–although, as the title of the story suggests, this "water" is not far from home itself.

The title of another story in the collection, "Tell the Women We're Going," could be read as the two men in the story informing their wives that they are taking a piss. The word *go* often brings together drinking, eating, pissing, defecating, and also sex–for example, "[. . .] shall we have a go at it?" (235) says a lover in the earlier story, "Will You Please Be Quiet, Please?" Like Hemingway–who often links drink, food, sun, water, and sex, for example–Carver keeps us close to the elemental and natural things of life. This pragmatic and experiential focus is in keeping with America's orientation.

Drink, sexual thoughts, and talk, especially in the form of questions and violent exchanges, do at times in the stories lead to the suggestion of new paradigms. The two couples in "What We Talk About When We Talk About Love," for example, arrive at what I take to be a moment of (troubled) transcendence at the end of that story.

"Gin's gone," Mel said.

Terri said, "Now what?"

I could hear my heart beating. I could hear everyone's heart. I could hear the human noise we sat there making, not one of us moving, not even when the room went dark. (154)

Despite the darkness, there is a realization here that they are, for worse but also for better, all in it together. The "human noise" stands in contrast to but is also a product of the drinking and speculative, sometimes aggressive, talk that preceded it. In "Cathedral," eating, drinking, and "cannabis" (366) become the initial means to discovery and bonding–and in that case, as in many others in Carver (and American literature generally), a specifically male form of bonding, the woman serving as the vehicle.

"So how you boys been keeping?"

Generally, Carver portrays marriage as a fluid and fragile state of being. Divorce is an ever-present option, and male bonding often circumscribes relations with a woman. "Everything goes," says the man in "Why Don't You Dance?", referencing the yard sale he's having of his and his wife's belongings (8). She has apparently left him. The girl in the story is disturbed "weeks later" by her decision to dance with the older man right there in his yard while her boyfriend, "drunk," dozes. The word *go* appears repeatedly in this story, too, in several forms, and meaning several different things: she asks how much things are "going for"; the television set, hooked up outside, is "going"; etc. At the very end of the story, as she tries to get things "talked out," she uses scatological terms to tell her friends about the experience: "'The guy was about middle-aged. All his things right there in his yard. No lie. We got real *pissed* and danced. In the driveway. Oh, my God. Don't laugh. He played us these records. Look at this record- player. The old guy gave it to us. And all these *crappy* records. Will you look at this *shit*?"(my emphasis; 14). The last part, "Will you look at this shit?" scarcely seems metaphoric. It's also worth noting that the story features an inadvertent case of male bonding: the boy sleeps while his girlfriend dances with another man.

The last story in that volume, "One More Thing," is typical of the "long line of low-rent tragedies" (156) we experience in Carver. In that story "go" is a reference to the practice of skipping school by the daughter in the family, Rae. She says that "no one could make her go" (156). Even the word *crackpot*–"You and your crackpot ideas" (159) Maxine, the wife, says to L.D., the husband–takes on scatological overtones (as well as drug overtones). Maxine wants L.D. out of the house (what he calls a "nuthouse"), but L.D. claims he has "no intention of going anywhere," only to say a minute later, "I'm going. [. . .] All right, I'm going right now" (157). I can't help but see scatological reference in this, too, and to see Carver laughing as he wrote it, just as I'd seen him, that first time, laughing as he emerged from the bathroom those many years ago in Santa Cruz.

Sexual fluidity and transference–and simple transportation to another location–often as a result of male homosocial activity, are also operative, and, if ultimately at times in service of connection, are regularly seen as demonstrations of disturbingly renegade male assertiveness and destructiveness. The discussion of Jack Kerouac's *On the Road* by Jay Parini, in his excellent study *Promised Land: Thirteen Books That Changed America,* is illustrative here. Parini writes of Kerouac's novel:

> ...Sal [Paradise] and Dean [Moriarty] hitch a ride back east in what they call a "fag Plymouth" as it belongs to "a tall, thin fag who was on his way home to Kansas." This car "had no pickup and no real power" and was called an "effeminate car" by Dean, who makes rude remarks about homosexuals, although he himself is unabashedly bisexual and had worked in his youth as a gay hustler–as he admits, even in the 1957 [published] version. (298)

The published version leaves out the man's homosexual advances, which Sal and Dean don't want any part of. But the intimacy between Sal Paradise and Dean Moriarty themselves is emphasized in the scene and throughout the novel. Carver's tale of Bill Jamieson and

Jerry Roberts in "Tell the Women We're Going," mentioned earlier, runs along a similar track. Bill and Jerry have been close, abnormally so it seems, since elementary school. They sometimes wear each other's clothes, even pants. They've "dated and banged the same girls." And "before their senior year, they chipped in and bought a red '54 Plymouth [. . .]" (57). All of this does not necessarily imply a homosexual attraction on the part of the two men, but it does suggest that there is something intensely homosocial in play. That is, while it's possible to read the story, as the title suggests, as detailing the boys, especially Jerry's, misogynist attitudes, I think the bigger if related problem concerns the intense relations between the males, just as it is the case with the philandering Sal and Dean. The "Plymouth" reference may be Carver's nod to the idea that buddy narratives (the only other novel included among Parini's "Thirteen" is *Adventures of Huckleberry Finn*) are central to America's founding consciousness—especially as regards two buddies heading out on the road together, without women.

The story raises questions about such close male connection at the expense of women—and maturation. The case is presented in a darkly comic brusque manner characteristic of Carver, and not unlike what we find in many frontier tales. Senior year Jerry drops out of high school and marries Carol. Bill has dated, and presumably "banged," Carol prior to Jerry's marriage to her. Bill then marries Linda, with Jerry as his best man. "The reception, of course, was at the Donnelly Hotel, Jerry and Bill cutting up together and linking arms and tossing off glasses of spiked punch" (58). "Cutting up," "tossing," and "spiked" all foreshadow the violent end of the story, and "tossing" evokes masturbation. The reception is at the Donnelly Hotel not only because it is most likely the only hotel in the small Washington state town of the story's setting, but also because we figure Jerry too had his wedding reception there previously. The boys continue their joint journey even into marriage. As in *On the Road*, the girlfriends and wives seem very much secondary.

The sentence that follows the reference to the Donnelly Hotel indicates, however, a change in Jerry which leads to growing distance between the two men—and a rather desperate attempt on Jerry's part to make things like they used to be. Jerry is getting ahead in life, at least in small town, middle-class terms, but Bill notes, "But once, in the middle of all the happiness, Bill looked at Jerry and thought how much older Jerry looked, a lot older than twenty-two" (58-59). A few short paragraphs later (it's now 1968 in the story and Bill is at Jerry's for a barbeque), Carver writes: "Bill was thinking how Jerry was getting to be deep, the way he stared all the time and hardly did any talking at all" (59). Talk, conversation, Carver suggests, is another and necessary condition and means to friendship and understanding. Jerry can't articulate the problem–from what he does say we can infer that he feels trapped by marriage and domestic responsibilities, and that his sex life isn't great. His physical gestures express his frustration best–and foreshadow the end of the story: "Jerry finished his beer and then mashed the can" (60). The two men decide to go for "a little run," meaning some more beers, some pool, and, with a little luck, some action. "'Guys got to get out,' Jerry said ." When they stop in a bar for some beers, the bartender, Riley, asks, "So how you boys been keeping? [. . .] So how you boys doing? Where you been keeping yourselves? You boys getting any on the side?" (60-61). Driving out on a rural highway, they notice two girls on bicycles. "I could use some of that," Jerry says. "That" being, among other things, what you can't help seeing when someone is on a bicycle. Earlier, at a bar, Bill had acknowledged the need for downtime. "Bill understood [. . .] He knew a guy's got to get out" (60). But unlike in Kerouac, the men will be expected home for dinner. Carver's characters are rarely in true transit. There's been a closing of the American frontier. The desperateness of Kerouac's male characters (of a somewhat earlier period relative to Carver) already suggests this.

We learn that Bill does not fully understand what's eating at Jerry, as the last two paragraphs of the story attest:

> Bill had just wanted to fuck [the girls]. Or even see them naked. On the other hand, it was okay with him if it didn't work out.

He never knew what Jerry wanted. But it started and ended with a rock. Jerry used the same rock on both girls, first on the girl called Sharon and then on the one that was supposed to be Bill's. (66)

Bill's confusion is also ours. Jerry's violent murder of the girls–significantly both girls–seems hard to square with just normal marital frustrations. The sentence "It started and ended with a rock" is especially enigmatic. There are various references to rocks in the story (and in many other Carver stories right up to and including "Cathedral"–an edifice made from rocks, of course, Christ the original rock). Earlier, pebbles are described as "flying from under the tires" (64) as the boys pursue the girls; there's a reference to the rock and roll of "Elvis or Bill Haley and the Comets" (58)–"Comets," more rock; and the central setting for the second half of the story is "Picture Rock." Further, a marriage requires a rock, i.e., a ring. A hard-on–"It started and ended with a rock"–is sort of a rock as well. The hard-ons set the boys off in pursuit of the girls. Jerry and Bill shared hard-ons in a sense, and in a manner suggesting the early sexual play of boys, in that they'd banged ("banged" also like the rock to the head) the same girls. The women seem almost incidental to Jerry and Bill's saga. Not that marriage is irrelevant: killing the girls perhaps gets Jerry hard in a way his wife no longer does. It's important that Bill is there to witness the killing: it is a perverse, indeed perhaps inverted, form of male bonding. But it is also a way for Jerry to reclaim his individual masculinity. An odd moment earlier in the story describes "Bill holding the door for Jerry, Jerry punching Bill lightly in the stomach as he went by" (58). Killing both girls asserts, or reasserts, an equality between Bill and Jerry, which Jerry appears to desire, but it may also point to one upmanship on Jerry's part, thus foiling such a desire.

One other rock is worth mentioning: Plymouth Rock. Carver has written, so it seems to me, an allegory of American buddy culture. When Bill and Jerry bought that Plymouth together they bought into

America. "They shared it. It worked out fine" (58). The first "it" in the sentence refers to the Plymouth, but it perhaps also refers to something not so definable–a cultural myth of America involving masculine independence and interdependence. Sal says that Dean's soul is "wrapped up in a fast car, a coast to reach, and a woman at the end of the road" (232). Cars brought freedom, especially for teenage boys (indeed America invented the teenager). But high school was perhaps the last time Bill and Jerry truly shared freedom, or women. In the end "it" didn't work out fine. It could be that the romantic intensity and potency of that early sharing blinded the two young men to time going past, and to the necessity, at least as regards Jerry, of maturing. Male buddy narratives don't end well generally.

"What are you doing?"

Male bonding in "Cathedral" is a happier occasion, if again perhaps not entirely for women, in this case our narrator's wife. She literally introduces the two men, her husband and her friend from the past, "the blind man," and on a metaphorical level she becomes the vehicle for their bonding, even the "cathedral" for their interaction. The ending of the story suggests possibilities for connection and of transcendence, but perhaps only for the men. Even when Carver deconstructs his text–most often and obviously through his use of talk–the longing for primary connection is nonetheless ever present. Unlikely communions, as critics have noted, are indeed possible. But they exist, when they do so, as an outcome of experiential and existential troubles, many of them fostered by relations with women. Indeed the male bonding may strike us as a tool employed by men at times to avoid dealing with women at all.

Characteristically, Carver opens the story with suggestions of menace. He wrote: "I think a little menace is fine to have in a story... it's good for the circulation" ("On Writing," 26). In the story, a husband, our first person narrator, directs his ire and uncomfortableness concerning the visit of "the blind man" to their house at his wife. "My wife," the husband repeatedly says, naming being a vehicle

Carver often uses to ask who we are and how we can know ourselves. "I waited in vain to hear my name on my wife's sweet lips" our narrator laments at one point, after listening to his wife and Robert reminisce, "talk of things that happened to them–to them!" (364).

The blind man predates the marriage. He himself has recently lost his own wife, "Beulah." "That's a name for a colored woman" (359) says our narrator, our protagonist–who is never named–as he seeks to get under the skin of his wife due to the discomfort he feels about having a blind man in his house, and, more crucially, attempts to deal with the envy and jealousy he feels since the blind man– "Robert"–and our narrator's wife shared intimate details of their lives in a manner we sense the narrator and his wife seldom do. Further, she continues her correspondence with Robert, via cassette tapes, after her marriage to our narrator, and, we learn, shares details of their marriage with Robert. Robert, "the blind man," is a kind of ubiquitous figure, even a mythic one, a listener and guide, despite our narrator's attempt to narrow or contain the experience of having his wife's friend in his house. Naming is part of a mythic apparatus in Carver. As with anything that's really good, even if rigorously realistic, there is a quality of a tale about it.

Carver's wife and fellow writer Gallagher put it well regarding his case: "This writer, Raymond Carver, had somehow managed to write in a multidimensional way that combined fable with what passes for that evasive surface called 'the real' to produced an entirely new entity" (103). A minimalist classic such as "What We Talk About When We Talk About Love," for example, is at the same time a story of surpassing allegorical and historicising beauty. The four characters sitting at the table drinking gin, in receding sunlight, enter a dream space, one in which, despite the contemporary setting, a discussion of medieval love lore is not only perfectly fitting, but also contributes powerfully to the ethical design of the whole. In "Cathedral," we again are made part of a discussion of medieval times. A mythic landscape offers an escape from and a remaking of romance and marriage. The loyalty of knights to their intended is brought into the discussion. In "Cathedral," the wife asked her husband to make her friend, the blind man, comfortable during the visit–to do so out of love for her. And, as I suggest later, the husband succeeds, if not exactly according to plan.

But just as naming adds amplitude, it also serves to raise empirical questions about identity and permanence. What's in a name? What is a "cathedral"? Naming becomes a trope for fluidity. Not only names, but also questions are central to this story–as they both are, we might note, to Whitman, the narrator's questions, "Do you have any idea what a cathedral is?" and "How could I ever begin to describe it?" (370-371) perhaps an echo of Whitman's *What is the grass?"* and "How could I answer the child?" Naming and questions are central to conversation; questions in particular are interactive and participatory. Talk is a kind of physical activity, immediate in addition to being teleological. And it is just such physical, sensory (often aggressive) activities as conversation which lead, in the stories, to a remaking of things.

That time I met Carver in Santa Cruz I remember him telling a fellow student writer, "I don't like your names." Carver prefers regular, unfussy Anglo names. But he also has a gift for the burlesque: "Beulah" (at the same time in may be an allusion to the Beulah in William Blake's "Milton"–Milton, the blind poet, we might also note). "Beulah" is attached not to a person but to a race, in the mind of our narrator (thus extending his stereotypes from the blind to blacks). He himself is brusquely called "Bub" by Robert. The fact that the blind man couldn't see a "colored woman" (though we have no evidence she was colored), or as our narrator speculates ribaldly, see that his wife might be dressed up in wild and mismatched colors, is of a dubious note in light of his total blindness (although later Robert reports that he has two televisions, one black and white and one color, and that he always turns on "the color set" (365)–which in a sense is what the threesome does later with the "cannabis," marijuana one of the means to new discoveries.)

Does our narrator know his wife without knowing her past? He knows of her divorce from her first husband, a young Air Force officer; "his wife's officer," is the rather snide appellation made by the second husband, our narrator. The officer was her "childhood sweetheart," the "first to enjoy her favors" so "why should he have a name?" (357-358). But of course he is named, if, again, in a more generalized, mythic manner, as "officer" and "sweetheart." There are marriage stories embedded in the story of the narrator's marriage. One of the stories we might call, in the manner of tales, "Beulah and the Blind Man," another "My Wife and the Officer," and another "The Blind Man and the Officer." "What We Talk About When We Talk About Love" involves four characters but references several couples and many marriages, past and present (Are we talking about love, or are we talking about what we talk about when we talk about love?) Nothing is ever free and clear. There are stories buried inside of other stories. Under such circumstances, how is transcendence possible? Our narrator's marriage in "Cathedral" is shadowed by his wife's experiences with other men. His naming of the other characters in the manner of a tales allows him to both distance himself and remake–rename–his wife's earlier experiences. In remaking, questioning, the narrator takes on an epistemological role–and a postmodern one. How do we construct stories about ourselves? What means do we use? Paradoxically, it is through visualizing the blind man's life as a blind man, putting himself in the blind man's shoes, so to speak, that our narrator begins to break down the barriers between himself and the visitor, and between himself and his own potential for feeling. "The blind man right away located his foods, he knew just where everything was on his plate. I watched with admiration as he used his knife and fork on the meat" (364), relays our narrator. Sight is presented as limited, just as are talk and naming; yet all–the narrator's chance to see an actual blind man, for example–are necessary means toward what in this story is the ultimate means to transcendence, that being physical touch, sensual engagement. An act. Indeed a mythic act. Myth provides a platform for wider experience, experience that incorporates not just space, but also time, the timeless, transcendent questions.

Just the fact that his wife had experiences that predated him is almost too much for our husband: "The tape squeaked and someone began to speak in this loud voice. She lowered the volume. After a few minutes of harmless chitchat, I heard my own name in the mouth of this stranger, this blind man I didn't even know!" (359). Food and drink, and later marijuana, provide for the initial breakthrough for our narrator and the blind man–men in particular often need a vehicle of some sort in order to communicate more freely (sports, for example). During the course of the evening, our narrator does indeed come to some knowledge and understanding of his position in the world–and perhaps beyond the world., to a frontier, an "elsewhere" often evoked by Carver. And his wife–specifically her body–is a central means to those ends. At one point the wife–who also is never named and thus more instrumental than individual–has "left the room," gone up stairs to "change into something *else*" (my emphasis), perhaps that being to a conduit of some sort. Meanwhile the husband brings out the dope. She returns "wearing her pink robe and her pink slippers" and asks "What do I smell?" (366). Her striking visual appearance along with the smell of the cannabis–and her?–sets the scene for pleasurable lethargy and mind- altering experiences. The atmosphere is now a warmer and more speculative one. "I shouldn't have eaten so much," she says, and the blind man suggests, "It was the strawberry pie." Our narrator says, "There's more strawberry pie." The connection to the pink-clad wife is hard to discount here, especially later when the husband, noticing that his wife's robe "had slipped away from her legs, exposing a juicy thigh," leaves it flipped open since the blind man can't see it, yet the husband adds, a bit menacingly: "You say when you want some strawberry pie" (367). He is still having his own dark fun, directing it maybe at the blind man, yet by this point in the story, especially under the influence of the pot, it seems more like pure fun and even an invitation to the blind man. Later in the story, when the two are drawing the cathedral on a grocery bag (another food refer- ence), and the blind man is "running his fingers over the paper"–just as earlier in the story, in a flashback scene, he ran his fingers over the then unmarried wife's face in order to gain some sense of what she looked like– Robert says to the husband: "All right, let's do her." She wakes, "her robe hanging open" still, and asks, "What are you doing? Tell me, I want to know." But the narrator tell us: "I didn't answer her" (373-374). He feels a bit guilty, apparently, and he feels as well that she wouldn't really understand–that is, it's so profound, it would be too difficult to explain in words. Activity, the doing is the important thing. He closes his eyes during the process of drawing the cathedral, telling us: "I thought I'd keep them that way a little longer. I thought it was something I ought to do" (375). "To do" is as crucial as "to go." He cannot name or fully identify the experience he goes through, with the aid of the blind man, at the end of the story. Carver appears to seek in this story something not unlike what John Worthen suggests about D.H. Lawrence, a writer Carver resembles in surprising ways: "The writer and the man wanted to discover new, post-religious ways of describing fulfillment: a state of self (or being) in which detached consciousness and body were not fatally divided but somehow brought together" (83). One of Carver's earliest efforts was an adaptation of Lawrence's "The Man Who Died" for the theater.

The men have drawn a cathedral together–Robert's hand on top of the husband's–in a simple, childlike manner, sitting on the floor. It is as small moment, but small things in Carver (short stories small things themselves) have particular explosive powers. The experience is "really something" (375), our narrator says. He means, I think, that whether it is fully identifiable or not, the experience is real, "something," and something beyond anything he could have imagined prior to the coming of the blind man to his house. Nor was, prior to all the eating, drinking, smoking, talk, and male camaraderie, on that single evening at his house–his cathedral–any thought of real connection considered possible. The domestic space is transformed. In this buddy narrative the men "get out" in a spiritual not a literal sense. The mythic, frontier landscape is brought home.

6

MISSING IN ACTION: VIETNAM AND SADISM IN TIM O'BRIEN'S *IN THE LAKE OF THE WOODS*

Midway through Tim O'Brien's novel, *In the Lake of the Woods*, Kathy, the wife of the protagonist, John Wade, is shown to us naked. She is, so this particular "Hypothesis" chapter speculates, alone on a little island in the Canadian wilderness, having decided to leave her husband and disappear into a new life via a small outboard boat. "When she cleared Magnuson's Island, Kathy gave the Evinrude an extra shot of gas and continued north past American Point and Buckete Island, holding a course roughly west toward Angle Inlet" (164). A few pages later we finally get what we–the narrator, John, ourselves as readers–have been waiting for, Kathy stripped down. The novel invites our voyeurism.

> She stripped off her sneakers and jeans, moved to the stern, hopped out into thigh-deep water. [...] Partly wading, partly swimming, she got behind the boat and wrestled it through the cattails and up onto the narrow beach. She used the bow line to secure the boat to a big birch and then lay back on the sand to let herself breathe.

[....................................]

For a few minutes she lay listening to things, the waves and nighttime insects, then she got up and took off her underpants and wrung them out. (171)

Kathy is apparently "alone" when she does get naked. And though she appears to be "lost" on "the Lake of the Woods," the novel suggests–at least at first glance–that she, in her aloneness, blissfully far from prying eyes, is able to commune with nature. Earlier in the novel she describes how the male-dominated political world and its "public eye" had made her "feel exposed and naked" (113), but now she doesn't just "feel naked," she is--and apparently there is no public eye. Unless of course she's being watched. By voyeurs, conspirators, witnesses? All of which I believe is indeed the case. Yet male scopophilia–I take the watchers to be of a male mindset--has a boomerang effect: at the "end" of the novel we see that John is also stripped naked, both literally and symbolically. As Peter Brooks writes, in *Body Work: Objects of Desire in Modern Narrative*,[1] "Time and again, these [modern English and French] novels reach moments when male desire for the woman's body unleashes a reaction in the realm of female sexuality that, by a circuit of return, marks the male body in a drastic manner" (82).

O'Brien's novel explores the full range of the problem--including both necessity and danger. On the one hand, the novel appears to argue that the debasement of John is a necessary operation to his finally finding his way home and exorcising demons, demons related to not just Kathy, but also to his father's suicide and John's participation in the Vietnam War. In order to cleanse himself of certain acts of killing he engaged in during his first year, John reenlists for an additional year. "'It's a personal decision,'" he wrote Kathy. [...] "I have to take care of a few things, otherwise I won't *ever* get home. Not the right way'"(147). Which makes a certain sense. On the other hand, we may ask if this is really the only right or honorable way home–should we trust John Wade on this matter? Doesn't it just lead to more killing? More time spent in Vietnam? Destroying the village to save it? And at the expense of his relationship with Kathy?

At the cost of *her* desires? Beneath John Wade lies a John Sade, I think. Though--more complicating still--the disturbing power of the novel rests in precisely Kathy's sometimes willing participation as well as ours in his, Wade/Sade's, profound games. Apparently, even Kathy can not forge or remake an identity--none of us can?--outside of such games. And, paradoxically, "home" can only be reached by those made new by loss.

The General Mathematics of Spying

Early on in the novel an overall voyeuristic context is established: as a young man, and even after return from Vietnam, John spies on his wife. He is intrigued by the mystery that is "Kathy."[2] He meets her in autumn 1966–"He was a senior at the University of Minnesota, she was a freshman" (32)–and by early November he's begun tailing her.

He felt some guilt at first, which bothered him, but he also found satisfaction in it. Like magic, he thought–a quick, powerful rush. [...] Finesse and deception, those were his specialities [...] In the evenings he'd station himself outside her dormitory, staring up at the light in her room. (32-33)

John has practiced magic since childhood; in Vietnam he is called "Sorcerer" by his fellow soldiers. The word "station" in the passage above invokes his military service (and oddly contrasts with the Romeo-and-Julietlike "staring up at the light in her room"). Though at this point in the narrative John has not yet been sent to Vietnam, he already appears a strangely suitable candidate for inscription into a world requiring "finesse and deception." Furthermore, John continues his reconnaissance of Kathy upon his return from Vietnam in a variety of manners, including actual spying on her. He is never quite sure of Kathy's commitment to him, and he is disturbed yet intrigued– as in foreign intrigue–by her life separate from him: "Down inside, of course, John realized that spying wasn't proper, yet he couldn't bring himself to stop. In part, he thought, Kathy had brought it on herself: she had a personality that lured him on. Fiercely private, fiercely independent" (33). We might question John's logic. Susan Hardy Aiken's comment on the male pursuers of Pelligrina Leoni in Isak Dinesen's novella "The Dreamers" is relevant here: "If [...] Pellegrina seems to turn men into dreamers, the text suggests that they are victims not of a woman but of their own desire and its constitutent fantasies, solipsistic mirror images that ultimately focus not on the woman, but on themselves" (56). Be that as it may, John is somewhat accusatory. "He understood her need to be alone, to reserve time for herself, but too often she carried things to an extreme that made him wonder" (34). He believes the spying is helpful. "No great discoveries, but at least he knew the *score* [my emphasis]" (34). Here, as elsewhere in the text, John reduces things to a kind of mathematics.

As Luce Irigaray suggests, male scopophilic tendencies involve covering as much as uncovering the female body: "*Veiling* and unveiling: isn't that what interests them [men]? What keeps them busy? Always repeating the same operation, every time. On every woman" (210 [my emphasis]). John's spying, his unveiling of Kathy, seems to both reveal and reconfigure the world: "In a way, almost, he loved her best when he was spying; it opened up a hidden world, new angles and new perspectives, new things to admire" (33). The hidden is now revealed, the world takes on fresh perspectives—but are we not also witnessing a process of reinsciption, revision? If Kathy were to stop being a mystery, would the work of thought stop? What would men do with all that time on their hands? And further, without reinscription, in a kind of new Vietnam of experience—John Wade's lost election, Wade's (like O'Brien's own) broken marriage—would O'Brien begin to forget too much, as suggested in one note in the text in which he appears to speak most directly as "himself": "My own war does not belong to me. In a peculiar way, even at this very instant, the ordeal of John Wade—the long decades of silence and lies and secrecy—all has a vivid, living clarity that seems far more authentic than my own faraway experience. Maybe that's what this book is for. To give me back my vanished life" (298).

But certain pitfalls are inherent to the recovery-through-creation operation "O'Brien" speaks of. John Berger, in his pioneering work on scopophilia, *Ways of Seeing*, emphasizes the way images actually replace experience: "Images were first made to conjure up the appearances of something that was absent. Gradually it became evident that an image could outlast what it represented" (10). Yet, as I suggested earlier, this remains a necessary operation. Paradoxically, only by being reimagined and reconfigured can one's "actual" experience continue to exist. Still, troubling questions persist. Do we reinvest and reimagine our own experience at the cost to someone else's version of events? At the cost of their autonomy?

The "Hypothesis" chapter in the middle of the novel at first glance appears to describe Kathy's escape–or possible escape–from the scheme of given things. Despite, and because of, the disorientation she experiences as she drifts further from home, further north, further into the night, the chapter elicits our identification with and empathy for her and movingly evokes a feeling that in water and woods she, a city girl, is in her element. Away from John, and the machinations of society–"No more politics, not ever again" (164)–Kathy appears to enter open territory; we sense her relief, even her physical release: "It was mostly open lake, wide and blue, and the boat planed along with a firm, rhythmic thump, the bow stiff against the waves. She felt better now" (164). It's as if she is making love to the lake itself. But "thump"? And "roughly"?

Do we not also remember that John is being accused, at least by some, of having offed his wife? The next few sentences are more reassuring: "The morning sunshine helped. Here and there she passed little islands with forests pushing up flush against the shoreline, purely wild, too isolated for lumbering, everything thick and firm to her eye. The water itself seemed solid, and the sky, and the autumn air. Like flesh, she thought [...]" (164). Yet "Like flesh" has a disturbing, if also exciting, ring to it.

And "Like flesh" begins to link up with "thump." "Like flesh, she thought–like the tissue of some giant animal, a creature too massive for the compass of her city-block mind," I take as referring not only to the woods and water, but also to John Wade's history, from the childhood he spent on or *wading* in the Lake of the Woods to Vietnam to his election defeat in his home state of Minnesota. The second para-graph continues the contradictory tonalities of the first:

> Kathy put a hand overboard, letting it trail through the water, watching its foamy imprint instantly close back on itself. Iden-tical, which erased identity. Or it was all identity. An easy place, she thought, to lose yourself. (165)

These sentences echo the opening of the novel, as they reaffirm its central, and disturbing, tropes of identity: sameness and difference; variety and repetition. While Kathy, in a later "Hypothesis" chapter, reacts negatively to the "dense, voluptuous sameness" of the forests (219), John mostly seeks sameness, a certain erasure of difference and distance. Spying denies separation.

Further, Wade makes the north woods into a kind of Vietnam. He even makes Kathy into Vietnam. Or, to put it differently, he hopes to erase his Vietnam experience by hiding it within the vast sameness of the north woods and of himself as indistinct from Kathy. And Kathy as him—when Kathy is in the wilderness, she is in John, that is, in Vietnam. Rather than escaping from John, she may be playing into his hands.

The Sadean Suggestion

Revelations about John's actions at Thuan Yen and of his attempt to cover-up his participation cost him his bid for the United States Sen-ate. John nearly succeeds in erasing from military files his participa-tion in the massacre of villagers at Thuan Yen, the infamous My Lai of Lieutenant William Calley.

> He went to the files and dug out a thick folder of morning reports for Charlie Company. Over the next two hours he made the necessary changes, mostly retyping, some scissors work, removing his name from each document and carefully tidying up the numbers. [...] Among the men in Charlie Com-pany he was known only as Sorcerer. Very few had ever heard

his real name; fewer still would recall it. And over time, he trusted, memory itself would be erased. (269)

But significantly, Vietnam is the one thing John can't erase. Yet has he succeeded in erasing Kathy? The chapter "What Was Found" tells us the following: "Nothing at all was found. No boat, no body" (175). John appears to have erased Kathy–and thus perhaps rediscovered her, and himself–by placing her in the context of Vietnam.

The northern forest landscape becomes a kind of equivalent Vietnam, a place where one's identity is erased, "an easy place [...] to lose yourself." John didn't know his way around Vietnam–yet perhaps found his true self there; Kathy is lost on the lake–yet perhaps realized something important about herself there. And we are also left to wonder if John is somehow making her go through a Vietnam-like experience so that she can know herself as he knows her. Her unfamiliarity with the outdoors is made clear: "For well over an hour she would've been lost without knowing how lost she was." (165).

Both the northern woods and Vietnam figure as liminal sites in which sunlight, in its power to alter the look and feel of things, dominates. The chapter entitled "The Nature of the Beast" flashes-back to Vietnam, describing it as "spook country" (103) (we also hear "gook country"), a place in which the senses, especially sight–that is, light and darkness, bright color, dreams or nightmares–govern. "The morning air was flaming up purple" (106). Sounds of terror and dying mix with light. "Sorcerer uttered meaningless sounds–'No,' he said, then after a second he said, 'Please!'--and then the sunlight sucked him down a trail toward the center of the village, where he found burning hootches and brightly mobile figures engaged in murder" (107).

Our narrator tells us later, describing John Wade at Thuan Yen: "The sunlight was in his blood" (109). And ominously: "At one point it occurred to him that the weight of this day would ultimately prove too much, that sooner or later he would have to lighten the load" (108).

Paradoxically, John can only "lighten" the load but making his married life into a kind of Vietnam, filled with light and darkness, gliding movement–and abrupt sound.

Sound–Expressionism's staple as sight is Impressionism's–is especially important in the mix. "The Nature of the Beast" chapter is followed by a "Hypothesis" chapter, which begins, "What happened, maybe, was that Kathy drowned." As though a mine or grenade has exploded, her boat crashes. "Maybe she was skimming along, moving fast [...] and then came a cracking sound, a quick jolt, and she felt herself being picked up and carried–a moment of incredible lightness, and unburdening, a soaring sensation [...]"(111). The word "unburdening," by pointing back to John's desire to "lighten the load," sets off a near echo that is characteristic of O'Brien's strategy of sonic suspension and ambiquity. Throughout the "Hypothesis" chapters we feel John's presence, and thus the presence of Vietnam, even if there is no evidence (except in the last two chapters, which focus on him not her) that he is actually there on the lake where Kathy has apparently disappeared.

Kathy, it appears, feels not just watched but pursued. Our low-guilt voyeuristic pleasure turns uncomfortably into a kind of sadism. We, like John at Thuan Yen, can't remain mere witnesses.

The "cracking sound" and "quick jolt," in the passage above, evoke Vietnam, just as, in a later "Hypothesis" chapter, which continues the "story" of Kathy's disappearance, such words as "flanked" in "She was in a wide, gently curving channel flanked by four islands" evoke military, as well as sexual, associations. Even the word "channel" calls up manipulative connotations, both in terms of to control by channeling in a certain direction and to control through magic or the occult. Are we inside some sort of torture chamber? The paragraph ends as follows: "The breeze had picked up now. Not quite a wind, but the waves stood higher on the lake, and the air was taking sharp bites at her neck and shoulders. There was no sound except for the rusty old Evinrude" (166). These "bites" evoke both masochistic and sadistic scenarios. But the sadistic implications are more powerful: is John, and even O'Brien, replaying Vietnam nightmares by putting Kathy through her own Vietnam-like experience? And are we readers--especially male readers–being asked to be witnesses to, indeed participants in, John's Sadean-like treatment of Kathy?

A culminating moment of the masochistic scenario comes when, after having stripped off her clothes in order to wring them out and dry herself off, Kathy, as the night and cold descend, "spanked(s) her hands together" (172).[3] Of course, Kathy is trying to encourage herself: "'Well, let's *go* ' she said, which gave her confidence." However, the hands here may evoke more sinister implications than even masochism. A few paragraphs further on we find Kathy reminiscing about her college days with John: "At one point he'd taken her face in his hands. He'd put his thumbs against her eyelids. "'Boy, do I *love* you,'" he'd said, and then he'd made a small turning motion with his hand, as if to drop something, and whispered, 'Girl of my dreams'" (173). In this passage there is not only a strange, and perhaps Sadean, slippage from "Boy" to "Girl," but also, and more important, the italicized "love" is played off against the italicized "go" of the earlier passage, the parallelism leading, once again, to a strange sense of John's presence, his omnipresence even when he is absent. "Well, let's *go*" becomes, through echo, the voice of John, internalized and ventriloquized as Kathy's "own" voice. And before saying "I love you" must John first put his "thumbs against her eyelids"? Is Kathy escaping? Starting over? "Get some sleep. Start fresh," she tells herself (171).

The scene continues: "For a few minutes she lay listening to things, the waves and nighttime insects, then got up and took off her underpants and wrung them out" (171). Wrung? "She put on her jeans, slicked her hair back, used the last slivers of dusk to do an inventory" (172). Slivers? "Kathy spanked her hands together." Spanked? "Right now, she thought, John would be getting a search organized. Helicopters and floodlights. A whole army of Girl Scouts beating the bush" (172). Where are we? "In the morning she'd start fresh. Find something to eat and fill up the gas tank and see what the day brought. Fresh, she thought"(174). "Fresh" even echoes "flesh," and horribly, "flush," from the opening passage of the chapter:

> Here and there she passed little islands with forests pushing up flush against the shoreline [...] everything thick and firm to her eye. The water itself seemed solid, and the sky, and the autumn air. Like flesh, she thought–like the tissue of some giant animal, a creature too massive for the compass of her city-block mind. (164)

An Elizabeth Cady Stanton-like image of a woman in a boat navigating her own course, as described in Stanton's "The Solitude of Self," is undermined at nearly every turn. The "giant animal" is nature but also, I think, John, Vietnam.

The Wade/Sade link appears to be consciously woven into the text. In addition to what appears to be a conscious effort to have Wade's name echo the name of author of the infamous texts on sexuality and pain, the Marquis de Sade, we learn that Kathy's middle name is "Terese" (9): throughout Sade's novel, *Justine*, Justine goes by the name of "Therese." References to Verona in the novel evoke a Romeo and Juliet scenario, but Kathy as Juliet also appears to allude to Sade's *Juliette*. While Justine is innocent and passive, Juliet is experienced and active: Kathy, we learn in the novel, is both Justine and Juliette-like, depending on how we read certain sections, and depending on how we take her relationship with John. On the whole we might say Kathy is less the innocent victim, like Justine, and more the plucky adventurer, like Juliette, than we may have first surmised.[4] Further, Kathy, watched by John, points to the power someone who is spectacle has over someone who is mere observer. Yet the fact that John prevents Kathy from having a child reinforces his often unfortunate, if perhaps unavoidable, power over her--and again it has Sadean overtones. As Camille Paglia writes, "Sade detests procreative woman.

Pregnant women are tortured, forced to abort, or crushed together on iron wheels" (244).

One further possible link between Sade and O'Brien is provided through Kathy's sister, Pat. In de Sade, Justine and Juliette are sisters. Pat arrives on the scene after John notifies her of Kathy's disappearance. Pat is presented as a hardened version of her sister: more experienced, more embittered, less idealistic, less romantic. She is more than a little skeptical of John's explanations regarding his role in Kathy's disappearance, but she doesn't come right out and accuse him. Pat and John wind up spending a good deal of time together, looking for Kathy. In one scene, in which John and Pat are alone together in a deep forest, possible sexual allusions are made by the narrator, which raises questions as to the nature of John and Pat's feelings for each other–though once again we see things primarily through John's point of view, which often means his fantasy point of view. The two of them have lain back on the ground to rest. "They looked at each other with the knowledge that they had come up against the edge of the permissible. Pat stood and brushed herself off" (185). The "permissible" has to do with whether they should discuss John's unusual behaviors, but the "brushed herself off" conjures up sexual scenarios. Even with Pat, John appears to playing some kind of seducer's game. Sade is known to have seduced his wife's sister. At any rate, the barbed exchanges between John and Pat, read a certain way, seem almost like lover's spats.

Following his election defeat, John Wade wakes to a world in which he is no longer the center of attention–even for himself. He is no longer a spectator to his own life; he can no longer dream, or be the same as he was before with the girl of his dreams.[5] In the opening chapter we learn that his life has all come "crashing down at once. Everything, it seemed. His sense of purpose. His pride, his career, his honor and reputation, his belief in the future he has so grandly dreamed for himself" (5).

In the opening chapter we see Kathy try to reassure John: "John, listen, I can't always come up with the right words. ... there's this wonderful man I love and I want him to be happy and that's all I *care* about. Not elections" (7). Indeed the emphasis on the importance of talking and on listening to each other is suggested, in the novel, as a healthy alternative to pure specularity. In the last three chapters of his study Brooks focuses on the movement away from visualization of body to the "talking" body as site of the "interlocutionary" (201) and, finally, as that which escapes signification. He points to a paradigm shift from seeing to listening.

But John and Kathy, much like Port and Kit in Paul Bowles's *The Sheltering Sky*, can never quite open up.

> On one occasion, as she was washing the dishes, Kathy made a low sound in her throat and began to say something, just a word or two, then her eyes focused elsewhere, beyond him, beyond the walls of the cottage, and then after a time she looked down at the dishwater and did not look back again. It was an image that would not go away. Twenty- four hours later, when she was gone, John Wade would remember the enormous distance that had come into her face at that instant, a kind of travel, and he would find himself wondering where she had taken herself, and why, and by what means. (16-17)

This ephemeral yet indelible snapshot of Kathy haunts John; it exists as an enduring image in place of and in the absence of some possible spoken exchange. Kathy suddenly appears, to him, as inhabiting a space beyond him, outside of him, outside of his perspective–if still within, but only within, his specularity. "The distance in her eyes. The way she rinsed the breakfast dishes and dried her hands and then walked out of the kitchen without looking at him" (17). And he wonders: "What if she'd spoken? What if she'd leaned against the refrigerator and said, 'Let's do loving right here,' and what if they had, and what if everything that had happened could not have happened because of other happenings?" (17) Kathy is apparently already off somewhere else, looking down into the dishwater but imaging other cleaner, more expansive waters. Or if one is to see her in a more negative light, maybe she is just not there for John now that their dreams are gone. In any case, it is perhaps too late for talk or loving within a domestic context. O'Brien suggests, finally, that we have to find a new way home–despite the cost to cherished notions of home and romance and even "individuality." Vietnam changed things.

7

A LAST JOURNEY OUTSIDE: ON BRIAN YOUNG'S *MOONIE* AND JENNY MUELLER'S *STATE PARK*

T wo volumes of poetry that appeared in 2017, while notable in their own right, also may be viewed as companion pieces. They are both particularly notable to me, since one, Brian Young's book-length *Moonie* (Fence Digital), is the work of my late (younger) brother, and the other, Jenny Mueller's *State Park* (Elixir Press), is the work of Brian's widow. The poems in Young's book and many in Mueller's detail a trip the two of them took in the summer and fall of 2010 across the Midwest and Far West. In an Afterword to *Moonie*, Mueller summarizes the trip:

> We headed to Wisconsin and Chicago [from St. Louis], then we drove through Iowa (inauspiciously colliding with a deer) and up to South Dakota. Badlands and Wind Cave. (Inevitably, we made a cranky stop at the Corn Palace, where we pondered our own corn-based fueling.) At Wind Cave we camped and rested several days. Brian starts the poem there on 7/10, then backtracks to 7/4 in Chicago. Then we drove into the Wyoming side of the Black Hills. ... In the next few weeks we drove as far west as the Olympic Peninsula, camping all along the way. (111)

A unique opportunity is afforded to compare two poets responding to some similar occasions–at least to the extent that any of us is in the same time and place as another. For example, Mueller acknowledges that upon learning two new words, *eyeshine* ("the look of eyes reflecting projected lights in the dark") and *bonebed* (used to describe a "heap of fossilized mammoth skeletons"), both she and Brian "grabbed the words for poems" (111). Mueller uses "bonebed" in "Recovery Act, the Black Hills" (4) to indicate a violent act of recovery while Young, who was already ill at the time, uses the phrase to refer in "Luna Lake" to the reduplicative act of writing–"the need/ to articulate, taken to this/ legal pad. My bone-bed" (7). Reading the two books in concert one does get a strong sense of, to employ the title of the selected poems by Lisel Mueller (Jenny's mother), what it is to be *Alive Together*, as companions, as husband and wife, as family members, as members of a certain (deconstruction-leaning) generation of poets, and, in this particular case, travelers toward, in more than one sense, a diminishing, yet ever-remembered frontier. All within the immediate context of the rise of the Tea Party, anti-immigrant sentiments, and fallout from the Great Recession. Young is witness to an invasion of viral forces–natural, commercial, and pharmaceutical–that appear to overleap biographic barriers, while a two-ness of observer and an observed landscape is fragilely maintained in Mueller. In both works, the sense of standing at the American frontier again is beautifully, startlingly registered. Young gets there by detailing piecemeal obliteration and replication and Mueller through soundings of descent and recovery.

Like most of Young's work, *Moonie*, "a poem in two parts," refuses as one commentator in *Poetry Foundation* writes of John Ashbery (Ashbery the master my brother sets himself against), "to impose an arbitrary order on a world of flux and chaos"–yet I will argue later the work is intended to be and succeeds at being a work that is all of a piece, made of many small pieces. A poetry of this and this, not of this and that or this that leads to that (the cause and effect philosophy Voltaire satirizes in *Candide*), and largely shorn of personal reflection is what we generally find in Young's work. Context, personal or otherwise, is eaten up, smashed, just as light in his poems eats up or smashes against the horizon. The lack of identifiable boundaries certainly raises the risk of solipsism. But such self-referentiality–there's scarcely a mention of family or even "Jenny" (Mueller more generous in this regard in her poetry)–allows for immediate, localized observation. Young adroitly marries the Ashberian meditative, self- referential tradition to traditions of social critique, employing satire or more relevantly perhaps, a post-romantic, punk-like desire to alter (altar) things, perform them, or smash them, as a means to the return of an original thisness ("no ideas but in things")–in *Moonie,* the separate thisness (species) of nature (if yet portrayed as mirroring one's own nature) seen as being under assault by various forms of social control and surveillance.

The title of his first book, *The Full Night Still in the Street Water* (Nevada 2013), might be seen as a modern updating (further duplication) of "the reduplication in the still waters of the tarn" Edgar Allan Poe wrote of in "The House of Usher." There is a turning in on and against one's self (like Poe, my brother was prone to substance abuse), but, as suggested already, it is a returning as well, a remaking, another turn of the screw. In Young's work, if less so in Poe, this involves a return to the natural world; but foremost for both writers is psychic adventure (Paul Bowles the writer who best understood that Poe was a sort of traveler). In particular, both writers enter landscapes chock-full of "'creatureliness,' to use Rudolph Otto's expression for a feeling of naked dependence on forces beyond the human scope," as writes Paul Zweig (173)–those forces such that even "iSeem cannot/pick up the signal," Young notes in *Moonie* (1) (iSeem–Industrial and Systems Engineering and Engineering Management–was our dad's professional field). *The Full Night,* if less directly than *Moonie,* employs travelogue actual as well as psychological, right from the opening poem "Head"–"And I'm still wearing the head/ that I picked up in the last country"–the word *still* comically invoking reduplication, specifically here America and Korea, respectively, or vice versa, or perhaps yet another country in between these two–to the penultimate poem, "Still"–"If we go on like this forever/ and to the hills" (84), the paratactical "and" implying that it might be a long journey indeed. Yet the volume's last and title poem suggests–despite its forward-looking final words "looking out the door"–a possible moment of respite from travel, psychic or otherwise (if still not from the Candide-like traveler's extra sight or thought, the "and" of things), Young writing, in a lyrical if humorous vein, "What was once surrender, i.e., gets off the horse and lies down in the autumn dust/ of maple trees" (85). We are reminded, despite Young's resistance to "reflection," as Bin Ramke rightly notes in a blurb for *Site Acquisition* (Fence 2008) (noting also the "devastating beauty" of "fierce looking" in the collection), that the description in "The Full Night" is of "a memory going down" (context–explicitly sexual in this case–removed in this later version, predictably). "The Full Night" is a recollection (suggesting a collective past, a bonebed), the word *recollection* appearing more often in this volume than one might have guessed upon first reading.

Site Acquisition further employs the extra thought dynamic, in poems that further and more darkly perform the task of describing an overtaken, self-mirroring landscape. In "Always Always Land," the last poem of the volume, the speaker associates his own drinking habits with the taking in of more and more land–the process all part of a "wolving brainwork." Such a disturbing acknowledgment calls forth on the part of the speaker the hope that the land will never become a "minefield" (which we also read as "mind-field," I think), but rather will remain "A mere outcropping of rock, a few trees, and/" (the extra and circular thought) "The absolute emptiness of our minds" (64). Some of the comic jouissance (indeed "surplus– jouissance"– Lacan) of Young's first collection is absent in *Site Acquisition,* the poems generally more broken up and open (if uniformly lit up–a "Flash Map" (4) as the title of one poem has it). The lines are more constricted, as if the poems themselves are construction

"Sites"; or even more minimally, as a central set of poems has it, "stilts"("Always Always Land" something of an exception). But even the minimal sites described can be taken as places to camp or rest for the night. "Stilt $8^{1/2}$" (no doubt part homage to Fellini's film) offers a compacted version of a camping trip. I quote here the poem entire.

> Outside of Inner Ovenbird licks up
>   Lives   all lies in   the animal
> Advanced in anti-coalescence   the animal will outer What's
> Her name? Our Lady of the Diagnostic Flame
>   Will only array   with the ingrate
>   Sun down downing the whole
>   Son already downed   Jenny and I
> Sleep in   Out here?   Before crossing over
>   To Outer Inska   with relevants
>   Peering out from   the opening
> Of the colossal   structure
>   That bears down   On
> Ward   Wired under
> World (37)

In the first line, Young is likely referencing "what to make of diminished thing" from Robert Frost's nature poem "Ovenbird." Things in "Stilt 8 ½" in their brokenness have become compressed, flipped, even slurred together: "will outer" suggesting both go beyond and come out and perhaps in replace of "alter" (or "altar," as the next line, "Our Lady...," suggests). Or in "Outside of Inner" or "To Outer Inska" (sexually suggestive?); or "sun" and "son"; or just in terms of sound, "Ward Wired under/ World." It's funny still, but in a darkly satirical way, for disturbingly things are already "Advanced in anti-coalescence" processes–"bleared, smeared with toil," as Gerard Manley Hopkins writes. While the poems at times may seem a tad too filmic, things blotted out, the lighting artificial, this descriptive strategy reinforces the sense of a chemical or electrical-like conspiratorial take over–"Ward Wired under/World"–nature itself, in Young if not so in Hopkins, part and parcel of the fearsome design. As is one's own sensory- registering mind.

Moonie was published as a digital book and includes Jenny's photographs and torn off bits of map. The photos are straightforward: Brian stands direct to the camera, hands on hips, feet splayed. In the background some big rock or monument. At the end of each poem is a date. Young's introductory remark, "I was a teenage moonie, and so are you," refers specifically to a brief period Brian spent in the Unification Church of Rev. Sun Myung Moon and more generally, I think, to a life as an outsider, in outsider places: he once described our family as always having resided in "the sticks" (cornfield Indiana and desert Arizona).

The volume is more accessible than much of his earlier work: indeed one reads *Moonie* as one might a journal or meditative sequence. The entries are more clearly firsthand, personal– sometimes too baldly or mundanely so. The rapid punk, breath-centered approach (Brian a big fan of Charles Olson) that works toward a collapsing of distance between expression and audience, gives way to some degree in *Moonie* to a failing sense of composition of any sort, i.e., a static jigsaw puzzle structure–"Chipped sidewalk old/ Puebloan, maybe Comanche, trucks ripping up/ the dawn" (36), an example of the suppression of "and" in favor of more direct juxtaposition ("ripping up" suggesting, in addition to rapid movement, tearing up or disposing of things.) There is less breathlessness and more room to breathe, due to a shortening of line length (Brian in fact suffered from COPD). In this work the next thought is not so much an extra thought as simply a next one–if still invasive (those "trucks"). At times dashes or an empty underlined space or on occasion just random letters leaves a thought unfinished. In the opening (and title) poem, "Moonie," Young writes, "Here, in the Foothills, in the tall/ prairie grasses, low between various/ wild flowers, and (once-again) invasive species, such as____" (1). The unfinished, offhand manner invites our participation.

This (deceptively) simpler style also allows for more direct commentary, the kind of accessible commentary Beat nature writers like Gary Snyder or a writer like A.R. Ammons permits. "It is in digression that one is most recognizable. And endless" (38), one such example. There are also astonishing moments of "natural" rather unenhanced description, as when he describes his fish oil supplement: "Looking inside, into what appeared//to be a hive of extraordinary golden/ honey bees, each distinct/ and clearly encapsulated, thinly clustered and still" (11). Many moments detail the business of travel and camping: "I woke up early/ and set to work./ Getting the fire/ started with a kindling of trail/maps & pharmaceutical/ brochures" (12). The incomplete or daily nature of many of the experiences, as described, paradoxically creates a more complete whole, as no one experience or day can be separated out as its own entity. Indeed *Moonie* leans toward the kind of totalizing space we associate with modernism. That is, while it is characteristically postmodern to suggest one set of words—or here one species (including as yet unnamed ones)—can fill in a blank just as well as another set of words, the number of "invasive" species we encounter here also has a cumulative effect, creating an overall moon-like landscape. We find in these pages, to name but a few species, mountain lions, bison, turkey vultures ("which interest me/ more than bald eagles" (17), the omen-like deer that "smashed" the windshield, prairie dogs, lady bugs, "unknown birds" (12), an "ochre butterfly" (13), rattlers, trout, and a praying mantis. The landscape itself is at times given animal features: "Reptilian visaged rocks" (31), for example. One might venture to say that these species have rather completely remade the landscape over into their own image, or that the reptilian area of the human brain has done so. Such circularity of mind and nature is a mode central to the American Sublime, given in this case a particularly westward, (re) pioneering turn.

Toward the end of Part One of *Moonie,* Young writes,

---------At 11,000 ft.
on the Williams Lake Trail

in the Mt. Wheeler Wilderness
we made a stop, a rest-stop.
I had a smoke
and Jenny an apple

After tossing the core
These birds quickly came to visit
First one, then 2 or 3 more
---- One finally did
find the core, and flew quickly away, while
the others hung around
for trail mix (49)

and goes on to describe a certain "Freedom of mind" felt in the "sky high peaks", if yet a freedom "Much like a wooden nickel"(50) (our dad often joking, "Don't take any wooden nickels"),

> but still
something that holds you, attentive
even ----
> Ready to light the fire
Put the sky in a drawer
for a while - - - There now —
> The Milky Way, but still

the mind at ease, somewhat
exhilarated even

even as he also acknowledges his mind, returning to again notice a "Clark's Nutcracker," is "not really free or empty" (50). Other campers, such as those playing "blackjack" from the early morning on, are also unavoidable, a bit of specific social commentary melded into a general sense of a things being "devoured ground/ barren sky/ boarded up" (51). However modern or sublime, the totality is yet a social totality. And ironically, the speaker himself is one of the invasive species.

In a short poem "The Hick from French Lick: Indiana Scenic Route," from her first collection, *Bonneville* (Elixir 2007), Mueller writes, "Brian, stop hitting those frogs...// Look out for that turtle unfurling its head/ swanwise in crossing pose." In this poem, it's Brian who apparently says: "'Ethno-mimesis, my ass." The speaker follows this with "Here comes that disgusting/ Hoosier jumper," a reference back to the subject of the title, French Lick's most famous son, basketball legend Larry Bird, but also—reinforced by the line break—jumping frogs, the poem ending, "drilled and perfected/ in HORSE. Who lets in rain lets the animals/out" (58). If Young's gift is for the eating away of things, detailing and collapsing them, at daybreak and nightfall—setting up camp and breaking it down—Mueller's is for watching from a certain height things unfurl, unspool, and lacing together with other things. Things held in, like the "animals," things held "so tight" (38), cluttered, or curled up child-like, are let out or spill out, and reconnect, "at a confluence" (59), where the headwaters meet, as in a dream. This is particularly so in *Bonneville*. "O'Hare Revisited" describes a child's grandfather circling "above and above, like a comet" in the speaker's dream, for example (39). In "Arsenal Rd."–"A moon gluts over Children's Hospital./ The moon puts on livery and corsetry,//begins conjuring, vocalizing–/ making operatic faces in a silent speech" (31)–we are witness to, from a certain dream-like, childlike height and distance, the silent stage business of violence and war. A "glass of air," as "Love Poem" (59) sadly suggests, is the sole place where people meet.

State Park seems to me a rich advance relative to Mueller's first book, as it is not so much an unspoiling of dreams or lit-up places, such as Bonneville Flats–"Well I skated toward a star/ on Lake Bonneville" (34)–but an unspoiling of feelings more grounded in the present, perhaps in part brought on for the poet by Brian's illness, just as earlier and in *State Park*, too, her father's death provokes such heartfelt responses. The sense of looking on from a height, and jumping and falling, plummeting, continues in *State Park*–in the aforementioned "Recovery Act, the Black Hills" kids are seen "jumping/ off cliffs by the dam" (4). Certain lines from "Peninsula" in *Bonneville* foreshadow the tenor of much of *State Park* (and appear to reference Brian): "Darling the campgrounds/ are sodden abandoned, their sites/ bitten in and the paths/ steeped in cold/ chemical soak" (4). Here the internal rhyme and the enjambment further an imagery which–if still dreamlike, ghostly, "abandoned"–is also more real than dreams, i.e., "etched" (4), unflinching, crucially linked to history and displacement (including President Obama's "Recovery Act," a stimulus package enacted to address the fallout of the Great Recession.)

State Park is dedicated "In Memory of Brian Young (1959-2014). The opening poem, "Landscape with Astonished Figures," begins as follows:

> Exactly at Bloomington-Normal
> the storm fell white-queening.
> My darling, I'm so sorry
> about these brute Decembers.
> Turned in, turned
> out of house, but do we want it
> any other way?
>
>   The storms keep come flying,
> "home in," 'til their object
> breaks them, but not entire.
>   We still have eyes, we still have
> voiceboxes. Cries we can raise
> over the tree of this park. To the breath
> expressed in their lacings. (3)

Winter is especially hard on COPD sufferers. The "My darling" here as in "Peninsula" signals a space right there before us, voiced. Sounded, like the "Doors slamming inside the surf" found in "State Park III"

(11). These poems take an inward Expressionistic turn–sound not sight the centralizing feature of Expressionism. Still things are also ever two, "Turned in, turned out," redoubled, criss-crossed, linked ("Bloomington-Normal"), "open, secret" (6), recovered–all the while not so much unwinding as in a dream, or a continuous journey, but falling down, sinking, homing in, in this poet's taut lines, like profiles, slim as aspens, each a yellow-tinged black and white postcard, indices in an audio file from trips outdoors. The voiced quality of these poems seems to encourage, and leave space for, a conversation. The often broken typography contributes as well to this effect. For example, in "State Park I," quoted below in its entirety, we readers appear to watch and point with the speaker, our participation necessary and even catalytic, compromising:

> going going
> while here the words flow
> (forth a negligible horizon)
> to where you are hard
> at witnessing the corner
> event (having borne
> yourself over the dunes,
> the reader, to happen it so) (9)

The word *hard* here suggests intense, possibly voyeuristic (perhaps untoward) attention. The word *negligible* sharing a root with "negligee."

However the watching and being watched central to these poems is not explicitly presented as it is in *Moonie.* Her concerns are not framed in terms of being directly invaded or monitored, but to being followed, escorted, shadowed. Things are not so much totally remade or duplicated as remodeled or renamed (sounded, echoed), "at syllable level" (39), often with subtly devastating results: "forest makes over to forestry" (4)–the school of Ecopoetics rising in the first decade of the twenty-first century in response to such concerns, i.e., not only the destruction of natural environments, but also their problematic management. Yet little is depicted as violently smashed or entirely merged in *State Park*: one poem begins with "2 searchlights: the moon/ and the border patrol" (13) while another, "County F and County H" begins with "Two osprey" (22). "And" is used to draw parallels, create balance, reinforce a two-ness. The writer's sobriety, lucidity, pastoral inclinations, femininity are at hand. There's more "we," less pure subjectivity (thus less pure objectivity)–it's more a matter of a fragile contingency, quiet endurance, reckonings.

The poems of *State Park* do not all address the specific trip Brian and Jenny took together in 2010 or their marriage. Gender roles, however, do figure strongly in several poems. "Nuns Falling down Stairs" begins as follows:

> Sound of water
> Falling through trees.
> No: it is wind
> sown with water's seed, carrying
> water's line. Each sex
> finds the other one crude,
> knuckles under. (27)

There are not so many animals or species in *State Park* as we find in *Moonie*, but there is persistent attention to "Only this form/ accomplished in shadows, female/ of the species" (27). A short poem, "Executor," is a response to Emily Dickinson's "My Life had stood - a Loaded Gun," as well as, perhaps, the role Jenny, a daughter but also a poet, plays as editor of her mother's uncollected work. The poem reads as follows:

> No difference in letter
> between killer and survivor.

> Emily Dickinson begged it—
> a question of "power" not skill
> posed in the place of the master. (46)

This poem is in its own way as packed and indeterminate (or nearly so) as Dickinson's. Does the speaker (and Dickinson) beg *for* it–freedom, sexual release, death–or does she skillfully beg the question when it comes the distribution of power between master and gun, man and woman, "killer and survivor," parent and child, artist and executor?

Some later poems in the book pick up both the marriage and the travel thread, indeed appear to be responses to some of the same particulars memorialized in *Moonie*. The final poem in Mueller's book, "Kohl," is a painstakingly etched plea. Her and Brian's different approaches to travel, relationships, and life generally, are made apparent in the last lines.

> Once I dreamt on a beach
> below ruins, woke when you came back
>
> from swimming, a dripping dark matter.
> The shore spread its hand, behind,
>
> knuckled with sun. And I know your critique of clarity
> has carried you for a long way,
>
> but now please it's time to turn back.
>
> If I line my eyes,
>
> will you stop smoking ("bearing all to the point
> at which we vanish," you said, writing

of ruinous churches.) Here is beach, here is bed.
Here is blazing

from which you step, impatient unscathed.

In these lines, the reassuring two-ness of "Here is beach, here is bed"
is so aptly, and heartbreakingly, laced with "Here is blazing."

8

GARDENS OF EDEN: A NOTE

Although Neoromanticism is a heuristic term, it also points to a literary movement, one that peaked in the 1950's with such writers as Lowry, Kenneth Rexroth, and Tennessee Williams. Two novels, remarkably similar to each other–Kerouac's *On the Road* (1957), cited earlier, and Vladimir Nabokov's *Lolita* (1955)–represent the movement of Neoromanticism into its proto-postmodern phase, in which the romantic subject increasingly retraces its ground, and does so discursively as much as narratively or lyrically. In Kerouac and Nabokov, despite their very different backgrounds, or in the poems of Frank O'Hara, for example, we see the telescoping of space and the discursive, often comic pause in mid-sentence so characteristic of the twentieth century's second half. These writers also signal a movement back to domestic themes, another characteristic of American literary works after 1950. Both novels happen domestically, in America, or really "America," a place which offers much of the world now lodged here in miniature, a replication of the larger world, yet one, in the 1950's, surprisingly homogeneous because the American Dream increasingly became a dream-factory. The itch to travel remains, but places begin to look a little bit too much alike, first like Middle America and later like California. Meanwhile, everyone is growing older and less innocent, as is the country. The wistful longing for one's youth and for the past, which we find so strongly figured in Kerouac and Nabokov's respective novels, or O'Hara and Ashbery's poems—a romantic tradition first fully realized by Whitman and extended by F. Scott Fitzgerald and others—suffers a new twist: one goes home to places that are in the process of being erased and surrealized. After all the traveling, one comes up against time.

The ghostly, liminal quality of Kerouac's seminal novel derives from a sense of confronting time—the end of youth—as the protagonists, with the help of speed and repetition, get lost in America, and Mexico. While getting lost or escaping to a countryside of one sort or another can clear space for the return of a dearly sought after childlike or godlike timeless state, it can also undermine one's sense of an adult self, especially as regards ethical responsibilities, as discussed previously. Sal Paradise in *On the Road*, not unlike Nick Carraway in *The Great Gatsby* as regards Jay Gatsby, shrewdly reveals the corrupt life of the novel's hero, boy-man Dean Moriarity.

On the Road and *Lolita*, or for example Kathy Acker's 1988 *Empire of the Senseless*, a later exemplar, suggest that the neoromantic, ethnographic story in the late twentieth century often is most successfully done as human comedy, as comic, if lyrical, burlesque. Works by Stephen Crane and Joseph Conrad, on through Sherwood Anderson, Ernest Hemingway, Henry Miller, Lowry, and Paul Bowles are important precursors. Hemingway is an especially central figure in the development of the modern ethnographic burlesque, though the burlesque side of Hemingway gets short shrift in terms of critical commentary, despite Hemingway's clear links to Mark Twain and Sherwood Anderson. Hemingway uses burlesque to reveal the conflicted underside of human emotional, sexual, and ethical life.

Hemingway's posthumously published *The Garden of Eden* spurred a new generation of criticism focused on gender bending and textual play in the novel and in Hemingway's work in general. But, for the most part, critics have yet to explore these manifestations in Hemingway in terms of genre and form. Hemingway is indeed going through a psychological crisis, one with a long foreground as critics have noted, but he is also having fun, playing with the genre of the burlesque. The play's the thing in *The Garden of Eden*. The doubling of persona, the use of non-responsive dialogue, the concern for life's transience–and the specifically Othello-like focus on jealousy and race–point to the stagey, indeed Shakespearean direction of Hemingway's novel.

Hemingway has always been self-consciously playful: "Indian Camp," one of his earliest stories, is ethnographic burlesque as its best, Stephen Cranian and Conradian in its violence and Ford Madox Fordian in its sexual underhandedness. The title itself, "Indian Camp," tips us off to its boy's camp hijinks as well as its burlesquing, campy intentions. Uncle George is smoking a cigar because he indeed may be the father of the Indian woman's child–a scenario that is in keeping with Hemingway's abiding interest in sexual triangles–but in lighting the cigar and passing out cigars to others George is playing his part in a stagey production about men and women, whites and Indians. The burlesque level of the story rather than undercutting the story's seriousness adds, through dark humor and parody, another level of awfulness. This awfulness is, I believe, found at a very basic level of the text. For example, the first page of the story repeatedly uses the word "in," possibly suggesting that Uncle George got "in" the "Indians." The camp skit continues, with the birth of the baby: "See, it's a boy, Nick," he [Nick's father] said. "How do you like being an <u>in</u>tern?" [my emphasis] In the end of the story, Nick and his father row away from the Indian camp, as if it were nothing that existed in solid reality.

But Hemingway is not, I want to quickly add, just making things up or just interested in how things are made up. While it is true that the way language works in the world is always a primary concern with him, ethical questions are also central to Hemingway, as the last scene of "Indian Camp" suggests: do Nick and his father have a false sense of security? Do they somehow manage to forget the Indians? Furthermore, the strong autobiographical element of the story contributes to its authenticity and intimacy. What neoromantics seek is real-life translation. What they hate is mere fictiveness. Mere formalism. Tim O'Brien succeeds where others fail simply because he was in Vietnam and not just some Vietnam of the imagination. And even he struggles at times, as in *In the Lake of the Woods*, to give "life" to the pervasive hallowed out feeling John and Kathy Wade feel post-election defeat. No amount of fictive play or formal, traditional storytelling will suffice to redeem a heartless, energyless–and ethically unstable–protagonist. At times the novel seems like mere performance, mere magic--what Lawrence, in his essay on Edgar Allan Poe, called "post-mortem" effects (77). Lawrence, too, is not untouched by such effects; indeed he explores them, especially through such characters as Gerald in *Women in Love*. But such effects, for all their interest, their truth-to-modern life feel to them, threaten the very survival of a neoromantic aesthetic. Tony Pinkney argues in *D.H. Lawrence and Modernism* that the choice is not between Joyce and Lawrence, as F.R. Leavis figured it, but between the expressionist *The Rainbow* and more modernist/postmodernist (and classicist) *Women in Love*. Pinkney chooses *The Rainbow*, believing that *Women in Love* prefigures a Samuel Beckettian world in which "witty evasions and blackly comic manoeuvres" attempt to evoke a bleak ontological condition but actually reveal, to that world's discredit, a lack of meaningful historical reality (109). I choose *Women in Love*, for both its modernist and what I perceive to be its expressionist's character, but I think his point is well taken. The danger is real. One might become but a mere postmodernist or new formalist and achieve, to use Pinkney's words, only "a desiccated formal perfection" (109).

As already noted, one postmodern development in the 1970's was minimalism. Hemingway is its chief precursor. To my mind, minimalism is often more successful than maximalist metafiction simply because most minimalism retains a realistic base (although Beckettian minimalism rarely does). This realistic base allows for ethical examinations of the various excursions into the unusual and bizarre so characteristic of the modern, as it simultaneously examines the realistic base and its norms. For example, Mel, a cardiologist and the central character of the previously discussed "What We Talk About When We Talk About Love", confuses the terms "vassels" and "vessels." This plays into the idea of vassels–but also knights and cardiologists–serving a vessel, that is, a Holy Grail which is, as legend has it, assumed to contain pure blood, purity and blood being Mel's chief preoccupations, but to, the story argues, his detriment (at least in his life outside of being a cardiologist). The fact that Mel has a real job, as a doctor, and a real ex-wife are crucial to the story's wide-ranging power.[2] Realism and enchantment work together, Garden-of-Edenlike. Indeed, as philosopher Jane Bennett argues, "the mood of enchantment may be valuable for ethical life" (3).

Of course the limitations of minimalism, especially in lesser hands than Carver's, hardly needs rehearsing–the label itself indicates its restrictiveness. Another recent literary development, also alluded to earlier, is New Formalism. It is a movement by poets who want to renew interest in narrative and formal verse and reestablish Western Civilization classical canons. W.H. Auden and Allen Tate are chief precursors. Auden is of course a great poet. Tate is a significant poet- critic. But both writers tried to go around Romanticism, via Christianity *and* Modernism, a journey which simply isn't possible, especially in America. It is perhaps relevant that Auden, upon moving to America in the 1940's, ceased to be a great poet whereas the romantic Thom Gunn, another Englishman, flourished. At any rate, the new formalists might do better to embrace, if not Gunn, then Philip Larkin before Auden or Tate. As a child and at the very end of his life Larkin was an Anglican–almost a new formalist requirement–but during most of his life, the middle of his life, he kept his distance from formal institutions (except libraries), and thus he allowed everyday pagan and romantic elements to grow in his work, including elements derived from Whitman and Lawrence and also American jazz. In America, one can't go around romanticism, so why try. And what is England but the country of the first neoromanticist, Emily Bronte.

So if not to Postmodernism or New Formalism, where do we look for the next phase, the next movement? We don't. In the end, the Anglo-American tradition is not one beholden to theories and schools. We don't look for the next big theory or movement. We look away.

NOTES

Introduction

1. Jack Kerouac was raised Catholic in a working class town. His trips west opened up a Protestant as well as Buddhist world to him, but he also appears ever drawn to Catholic strongholds such as San Francisco and Mexico. Kerouac was a great admirer of the James Joyce, in part no doubt due to Joyce's baroque, catholic style; in part also, one surmises, due to Joyce's working class background.

1. The Greater Body: D.H. Lawrence's *The Plumed Serpent*

1. Several critics, among them Walter Allen and Malcolm Bradbury, have traced Lowry's work to Joyce, Faulkner, and Conrad, that is, to High Modernism. "The Joycean echoes are strong: the novel [*Under the Volcano*] is set on a single day, depends on a complex management of consciousness, functions through a variety of styles, and each chapter is structured to a set of complex codes," writes Bradbury in *The Modern English Novel* (New York: Penquin, 1994), p. 301. However, a different line of influences, from Hardy to Lawrence, was also important to Lowry. Lowry acknowledged Lawrence as his chief precursor and went to great lengths to literally retrace Lawrence's steps in both Europe and North America. More importantly, while Lowry does employ a kind of high modernist lyricism in his work, he rarely entirely dissolves tensions between narrative and poetry, action and word, sense and sound, as high modernists often do. In his "Introduction" to *Under the Volcano* (Plume),

Stephen Spender discusses both Lowry's adoration for and rejection of High Modernism.

2. Quest and Presdestination in Paul Bowles's *The Sheltering Sky*

1. Joyce Carol Oates was perhaps the first to comment on the sense of predestination in Bowles. See *The Profane Art: Essays and Reviews* (New York: Dutton, 1983).

2. Alexandria as city and controlling metaphor is Durrell's primary interest in *The Alexandria Quartet,* but it still seems odd to me that his characters never, or almost never, think in terms of salvation lying in the deserts outside the city. But perhaps that is precisely Durrell's point.

3. Richard Patteson's argument that Port and Kit "expose themselves in this way [to the primitive] not so much from a desire for self-destruction as, paradoxically, from a longing for self-preservation" (xii) is close to my own argument in *The World Outside: The Fiction of Paul Bowles* (Austin: University of Texas P, 1987).

4. Bernardo Bertolucci, who directed a film version of *The Sheltering Sky,* also took up this theme in an earlier work, *The Last Tango in Paris.*

5. The presence of typical Romantic structures and transactions in Modernist and Late Modernist poetry (juxtapositions of observer/landscape, house/ nature, ship/sea images, with significant interactions between contrasted halves) demonstrates how Romantic themes continue in some sense to be our given," writes James Applewhite in *Seas and Inland Journeys* (Athens: University of Georgia P, 1985), p. vii.

3. Self-Portraits in Space and Time: Robert Lowell and John Ashbery

1. Interestingly, Lawrence's objection to Whitman's adhesiveness, in *Classic Studies in American Literature,* is very much like the following objections by Sigmund Freud, in *Civilization and Its Discontents,* to Saint Francis and others who tout an "all-embracing love of others and of the world at large": "A love that does not discriminate seems to us to lose some of its value, since it does an injustice to its object. And secondly, not all men are worthy of love."

2. John Willett's description of German Expressionism might be applied to Lowell, especially early Lowell: "darkness, introspection, a concern with the

mysterious and uncanny, massive metaphysical speculation, a certain gratuitous cruelty and a brilliant linear hardness, expressed sometimes by the most extravagant convolutions" See *Expressionism* (New York: McGraw-Hill, 1970), p. 45.

3. See Herbert Schneidau's *Waking Giants* (London: Oxford UP, 1991) for a different take on Gretta's love for Michael Furey. I agree with him that Michael is a somewhat pallid romantic figure, but I don't believe Joyce intended her love for Michael to signify "the worshipped corpse, used in Ireland to throttle the spirit of life in favor of sterile sentimentality" (9).

4. Grammatical parallels to such a scheme might be organized as follows: God-Definite Article; King- Noun; Nation-Verb; Self-Indefinite Article; Language-Preposition. Lowell thus inhabits a Nation-Verb, Self-Indefinite Article matrix, while Ashbery lives in the Self-Indefinite Article, Language-Preposition matrix. Stevens was perhaps the first poet to make the preposition so central to his syntax, which resulted in extensiveness and abstractness.

5. Some interesting parallels might also be drawn to the work of "new realist" Raymond Carver. His "What We Talk About When We Talk About Love" within its relatively few pages paints a miniature history of love (from at least the time of medieval knights forward) and explores the painful distance which lies between one's self and one's former, as well as current, lovers.

4. Traveling through the Dark: William Stafford and the Surrealism of the Far West

1. Theodore W. Adorno in "Looking Back on Surrealism," in *Literary Modernism*, ed. by Irving Howe (New York: Fawcett, 1967), argues that in surrealism the "subject, grown absolute, legislating freely for itself, and liberated from any concern for the empirical world, reveals itself in the face of complete depersonalization as inanimate and virtually dead, which throws it completely back upon itself and its protest. The dialectic of subjective freedom in a situation of objective unfreedom. ... In as much as they [surrealists] arrange the archaic they create *nature morte*. These pictures are not so much those of an inner essence rather they are object-fetishes on which the subjective, the libido, was once fixated. They bring back childhood and not by self-submersion" (222-223). Both Corso and Hugo had difficult child-

hoods. Corso, whose favorite poet is Poe, is particularly death-obsessed in his work.

5. Men, Menace, and Transcendence in Raymond Carver

1. *Beginners: The Original Version of What We Talk About When We Talk About Love,* published subsequently to *What We Talk About When We Talk About Love,* suggests that the scatological direction of the final version was heavily influenced by the editorial influence of Gordon Lish.

2. William Inge is often taken as a recorder of the lives of small-town folk of the American Midwest, in a realist, if colorful manner. In his plays we meet the local doctor, the schoolteacher, traveling salesmen, waitresses, many housewives, their lives enlivened but generally not overthrown by an outsider or sophisticate who appears on the scene. But it would be missing a key element of Inge's art should we not pay attention to the repressed dreams of his locals, and in particular the way in which these repressed dreams and desires, especially upon the arrival of an outsider, cast a kind of spell on the respective localities. Inge is formally concerned with the conflict between illusion and reality. The lines between the daily roles William Inge's people play in their small town and the roles they play as characters in the dream-landscape of his plays is smudged. Playacting--"the game of roleplaying," as Luigi Pirandello put it in his play *Six Characters in Search of an Author* (which concerns six living characters--family members embroiled in their own human drama--who come to a theater and demand that the manager and his actors stage their life story) is key to his plays, as it is key to small town (or neighborhood) life in particular since people are known for what they do more than by who they are (when you meet people in urban and especially suburban settings you generally don't at first know what they do, it being wrong, for instance, to assume a woman is a stay-at-home mother). Inge's people are identified as a father, a mother, a daughter, someone's daughter, someone's little brother, etc. (not unlike in Pirandello)--the encounters more personal because you see these folk on a regular basis and in a variety of capacities (at school, the grocery store, church, ballfields), but also abstract as they are identified as belonging to a certain set of people and as performing a certain role in the town's affairs (although unlike in the more politically minded Ibsen, we

never get to see town officials). Raymond Carver, a new realist in a manner we might liken to Inge (the comparison furthered by the dialogue-driven, dramatic, rather than narrative, inclinations of Carver's stories), also finds it useful to identify his characters in a typological minimalist fashion as, for instance, the baker, only to, like Inge, undermine such simple designations.

6. Vanishing Point: Sadism in Tim O'Brien's *In the Lake of the Woods*

1. Coincidentally, O'Brien's strip scene takes place near the middle of his novel just as Brooks places an open crotch shot, reproduction of Gustave Courbet's *L'origine du Monde,* right in the middle of his text. Brooks's text is a striptease, working toward such later chapters as "Nana at Last Unveil'd."

2. In *Empire of the Senseless* (New York: Grove Weidenfeld, 1988), Kathy Acker writes, 'All I know is that we have to reach this construct. And her name's Kathy' (34). The postmodern and flesh-focused nature of O'Brien's novel suggest he may have had Acker's "Kathy" in mind.

3. Kathy stripping strongly echoes a scene from Ernest Hemingway's *A Farewell to Arms* (New York: Scribner's, 1929) in which Frederic Henry strips while on the run from Italian forces: "I took off my trousers and wrung them too, then my shirt and under clothing. I *slapped and rubbed* myself and then dressed again" [my emphasis](227). The change of gender is perhaps significant. Toward the end of the novel, John strips, diving into the water in search of Kathy (242).

4. Kathy is in many respects like Mary Anne Bell, from O'Brien's *The Things They Carried* (New York: Penquin, 1991), who just shows up in Vietnam, ostensibly to visit her boyfriend but in fact to experience the war. Mary Anne Bell also disappears, joins the missing. "She had crossed to the other side. She was part of the land. She was wearing her culottes, her pink sweater, and a necklace of human tongues. She was dangerous. She was ready for the kill" (125).

5. Perhaps John's desire "to be loved" is really more about pride. Rene Girard writes in *Resurrection from the Underground: Feodor Dostoevsky* (New York: Crossroad, 1997): "Pride seeks to prove that it can gather and unify everything real around itself. ... Masochism and sadism mirror the romantic nostalgia for lost unity, but this nostalgia is mingled with pride. Far from disintegrat-

ing, the desire it produces rather disperses, for it wanders always toward the Other" (63).

8. Gardens of Eden: A Note

1. Graham Greene is another mid-century writer who places work and jobs at the center of his fiction. Greene's protagonists are likely to be defined by their job. Even when the protagonist is a writer, as in *The Quiet American* or *The End of the Affair,* he is a working writer who struggles to support himself with his pen. His writers take on their work with a sense of being a practitioner, someone duty-bound. They must work. And not so much in the Hemingway sense of working at writing because nothing else makes sense, but as way of fully participating in the social culture of work, of survival, of class burden. His characters, writers and others–policemen, priests, hotel owners, and other workers–are on their own in an existential fashion, like in both Hemingway and Kerouac, for example, but Greene's protagonists are not so existential as to be outside the social market-place. In other words, while they are assigned (or have after a fashion assigned themselves) to some colonial (exotic) outpost, they mix in the general and not the bohemian scene.

WORKS CITED

Introduction.
Poirier, Richard. 1966. *A World Elsewhere.* New York: Oxford. Wilson, Edmund. 1931. *Axel's Castle.* New York: Scribner's.

1. The Greater Body: D.H. Lawrence's *The Plumed Serpent*
Barthelme, Donald. *The Dead Father.* 1975. New York: Farrar, Straus and Giroux. Barthes, Roland. 1975. *The Pleasure of the Text.* New York: FarrerStraus and Giroux.

Baudrillard, Jean. 1983. "What Are You Doing After the Orgy?" Art Forum XXII, No. 2: 42-46. Beckett, Samuel. *Worstword Ho.* London: John Calder, 1983.

Boyle, T. Coraghessan. 1985. *Greasy Lake and Other Stories.* New York: Viking.

Clark, L.D. 1989. "Making the Classic Contemporary." *D.H. Lawrence in the Modern World.* Ed. Peter Preston and Peter Hoare. London: Macmillan.

Clark, L.D. 1980. *The Minoan Distance.* Tucson: University of Arizona.

Hannah, Barry. 1985. *Airships.* New York: Random House.

Hassan, Ihab. 1982. *The Dismemberment of Orpheus*, 2nd Ed. Madison: University of Wisconsin. Honig, Edwin. 1959. *Dark Conceit: The Making of Allegory.* Evanston: Northwestern UP. Lawrence, D.H. 1978. "A Propos of Lady Chatterly's Lover." *Phoenix II.* New York: Penquin.

____. *Etruscan Places.* New York: Viking, 1957.

____. 1972. "Indians and an Englishman." Phoenix. New York: Viking, 1972.

____. 1972. "Introduction to These Paintings." *Phoenix*. New York: Viking.

____. 1951. *The Plumed Serpent*. New York: Alfred A. Knopf.

____. 1960. *Women in Love*. New York: Viking.

McCaffery, Larry, and Linda Gregory, eds. 1987. "Barry Hannah." *Alive and Writing: Interviews with American Writers of the 1980's*. Urbana: University of Illinois: 111-125. Ortega y Gasset, Jose. 1960. *What is Philosophy?* New York: Norton. Parmenter, Ross. 1984. *Lawrence in Oaxaca*. Salt Lake City:Peregrine Smith.

Rothenberg, Jerome. 1988. "American Indian Poetry and the 'Other' Traditions." *American Literature*. London: Penguin.

Sontag, Susan. 1980. "Approaching Artaud." *Under the Sign of Saturn*. New York: Farrar, Straus, and Giroux.

Wilson, Edmund. 1931. *Axel's Castle*. New York: Scribner's, 1931.

2. Quest and Predestination in Paul Bowles's *The Sheltering Sky*

Anderson, Sherwood. 1949. *The Portable Sherwood Anderson*. Ed. Horace Gregory. New York: Viking. Barth, John. 1994. Interview. *Chicago Review* 40.4.

Bataille, Georges. 1987. *Story of the Eye*. Trans. Joachim Neugroschel. San Francisco: City Lights.

Bokenkotter, Thomas. 1979. *A Concise History of the Catholic Church*. Revised Edition. New York: Doubleday.

Bowles, Paul. 1983. *Coversations with Paul Bowles*. Ed. Gena Dagel Caponi. Jackson: UP of Mississippi.

____. 1966. *The Delicate Prey*. New York: Ecco.

____. 1985. *Let It Come Down*. Santa Barbara: Black Sparrow.

____. 1981. *Midnight Mass*. Santa Rosa: Black Sparrow, 1989.

____. 1990. *The Sheltering Sky*. International Ed. New York: Vintage.

____. 1966. *Up Above the World*. New York: Ecco.

____. 1972. *Without Stopping*. New York: Ecco.

Caponi, Gena Dagel. 1994. *Paul Bowles: Romantic Savage*. Carbondale: Southern Illinois UP.

Donoghue, Denis. 1987. *Reading America*. University of California P.

Durrell, Lawrence. 1957. *Justine*. New York: Dutton.

Eberhardt, Isabelle. 1975. *The Oblivion Seekers*. Trans. Paul Bowles. San Francisco: City Lights.

Green, Michelle. 1991. *The Dream at the End of the World: Paul Bowles and the Literary Renegades in Tangier*. New York: HarperCollins.

Hollander,John. 1998. *Melodious Guile: fictive pattern in poetic language*. New Haven: Yale UP.

Hibbard, Allen. 1993. *Paul Bowles: A Study of the Short Fiction*. New York: Twayne.

Kazin, Alfred. 1997. *God and the American Writer*. Vintage.

Lawrence, D.H. 1971. *Studies in Classic American Literature*. New York: Viking.

Paglia, Camille. 1991. *Sexual Personae*. New York: Vintage.

Perloff, Margorie. 1983. *The Poetics of Indeterminacy*. Evanston, IL: Northwestern UP.

Pounds, Wayne. 1985. *Paul Bowles: The Inner Geography*. New York: Peter Lang.

Said, Edward. 1979. *Orientalism*. New York: Vintage.

Schneidau, Herbert. 1991. *Waking Giants*. New York: Oxford UP.

Smith, Huston. 1965. *The Religions of Man*. New York: Harper and Row.

Stewart, Lawrence D. 1974. *Paul Bowles: The Illumination of North Africa*. Carbondale: Southern Illinois UP.

Tarnas, Richard. 1991. *The Passion of the Western Mind*. New York: Harmony.

3. Self-Portraits in Time and Space: Robert Lowell and John Ashbery

Ashbery, John. 1970. *The Double Dream of Spring*. New York: E.P. Dutton.

____. 1992. *Flow Chart*. New York: Knopf.

____. 1981. *Reported Sightings: Art Chronicles, 1975-1987*. Ed. David Bergman. Cambridge, MA: Harvard UP.

____. 1975. *Self-Portrait in a Convex Mirror*. New York: Viking.

Axelrod, Steven Gould. 1978. *Robert Lowell: Life and Art*. Princeton: Princeton UP.

Bloom, Harold, ed. 1986. *Contemporary Poets*. New York: Chelsea House.

Crase, Douglas. 1985. "The Prophetic Ashbery." *John Ashbery*. Ed. Harold Bloom. New York: Chelsea. 127-43.

Cohen, Keith. 1980. "Ashbery's Dismantling of Bourgeois Discourse." *Beyond Amazement: New Essays on John Ashbery*. Ed. David Lehman. Ithaca, N.Y.: Cornell UP.

Gray, Richard. 1980. *American Poetry of the Twentieth Century.* London: Longman.

Kalstone, David. 1977. *Five Temperaments.* New York: Oxford UP.

Kaplan, Robert D. 1994. "The Coming Anarchy." *Atlantic Monthly* Feb.: 44-76.

Lowell, Robert. 1973. *History.* New York: Farrar, Straus and Giroux.

____. 1964. *Life Studies and For the Union Dead.* New York: Farrar, Straus and Giroux.

Nathanson, Tenney. 1992. *Whitman's Presence.* New York: New York UP.

Shetley, Vernon. 1993. *After the Death of Poetry.* Durham: Duke UP.

4. Traveling through the Dark: William Stafford and the Surrealism of the Far West

Altieri, Charles. 1979. *Enlarging the Temple.* Lewisburg: Bucknell UP.

____. 1984. *Self and sensibility in contemporary American poetry.* Cambridge: Cambridge UP.

Berryman, John. 1962. *Stephen Crane.* New York: Farrar, Straus,Giroux.

Breslin, James E.B. 1984. *From Modern to Contemporary: American Poetry 1945-1965.* Chicago: University of Chicago P.

Corso, Gregory. 1989. *Mindfield.* New York: Thunder's Mouth.

Eliot, T.S. 1969. *The Complete Poems and Plays.* London: Faber and Faber.

Ginsberg, Allen. 1956. *Howl.* San Fransico: City Lights.

Hugo, Richard. 1984. *Making Certain It Goes On: Collected Poems.* New York: W.W. Norton.

Kerouac, Jack. 1959. *The Dharma Bums.* New York: Viking.

Marvell, Andrew. 1972. *The Complete Poems.* Ed. Elizabeth Story Donno. Middlesex, England: Penguin.

O'Hara, Frank. 1974. *Selected Poems.* Ed. Donald Allen. New York: Random House.

---. 1975. *Standing Still and Walking in New York.* Bolinas, CA: Grey Fox.

Stafford, William. 1993. *The Darkness Around Us Is Deep: Selected Poems.* Ed. Robert Bly. New York: Harper and Row.

---. 1991. *Passwords.* New York: Harper and Row.

Stitt, Peter. 1995. "William Stafford's Wilderness Quest." *On William Stafford.* Ed. Tom Andrews. Ann Arbor: University of Michigan P.

Van Ghent, Dorothy. 1961. "Comment." *A Casebook on the Beats.* Ed.Thomas Parkinson. New York: Thomas Y. Crowell.

5. Men, Menace and Transcendence in Raymond Carver

Carver, Raymond. "Interview." *Writers at Work: The Paris Review Interviews*, 7th Series, edited by George Plimpton, Penguin, 1986, pp. 299-327.

____. "Cathedral." *Where I'm Calling From*, Vintage, 1989, pp. 356-375.

____. "On Writing." *Fires*, Vintage, 1989, pp.22-27.

____. "One More Thing." *What We Talk About When We Talk About Love*, Vintage, 1989, pp. 155-159.

____. "So Much Water So Close to Home." *What We Talk About When We Talk About Love*, Vintage, 1989, pp. 79-88.

____. "Tell the Women We're Going." *What We Talk About When We Talk About Love*, Vintage, 1989, pp. 57-66.

____. "A StoryTeller's Shoptalk." *New York Times on the Web*, New York Times, 10 March 2016, www.nytimes.com.

____. "What We Talk About When We Talk About Love." *What We Talk About When We Talk About Love*, Vintage, 1989, pp. 137-154.

____. "Why Don't You Dance?" *What We Talk About When We Talk About Love*, Vintage, 1989, pp. 3- 10.

____. "Will You Please Be Quiet, Please." *Will You Please Be Quiet, Please*, McGraw-Hill, 1978, pp. 225-249.

Gallagher, Tess. "The Ghosts of Dreams." *Remembering Ray*, edited by William L. Skull and Maureen P. Carroll, Capra Press, 1993, pp. 103-107.

Greenspan, Ezra. "Some Remarks on the 'Participle-Loving Whitman.'" *The Cambridge Companion to Walt Whitman*, edited by Ezra Greenspan, Cambridge UP, pp. 92-109.

Parini, Jay. *Promised Land: Thirteen Books That Changed America*, Anchor, 2010.

Worthern, John. D.H. Lawrence: *The Life of an Outsider*, Penguin, 1991.

6. Vanishing Point: Sadism in Tim O'Brien's *In the Lake of the Woods*

Aiken, Susan Hardy. 1990. *Isak Dinesen and the Engendering of Narrative*. Chicago: University of Chicago P.

Berger, John. 1972. *Ways of Seeing*. London: Penquin.

Brooks, Peter. 1993. *Body Work: Objects of Desire in Modern Narrative.* Cambridge, MA: Harvard UP.

Irigaray, Luce. 1985. *This Sex Which Is Not One.* Trans. Catherine Porter with Carolyn Burke. Ithaca, N.Y.: Cornell UP.

O'Brien, Tim. 1995. *In the Lake of the Woods.* New York: Penquin. Paglia, Camille. 1991. *Sexual Personae.* New York: Vintage.

7. A Last Journey Outside: On Brian Young's Moonie and Jenny Mueller's *State Park*

Mueller, Jenny. *Bonneville.* Denver: Elixer Press, 2007.

____. *State Park.* Denver: Elixer Press, 2017.

"Remembering John Ashbery." Poetry Foundation. *Poetry Foundation.org.* 2019.

Young, Brian. *The Full Night Still in the Street Water.* Reno: University of Nevada Press, 2003.

____. *Moonie.* Albany, NY: Fence Digital, 2017.

____. *Site Acquisition.* Albany, NY: Fence, 2008.

Zweig, Paul. *The Adventurer.* New York: The Akadine Press, 1999.

Conclusion: Gardens of Eden

Bennett, Jane. 2001. *The Enchantment of Modern Life.* Princeton: Princeton U.P.

Lawrence, D.H. 1964. *Studies in Classic American Literature.* New York: Viking.

Pinkney, Tony. 1990. *D.H. Lawrence and Modernism.* Iowa City: University of Iowa P.

AUTHOR INDEX

Fitzgerald, F. Scott, 123, 124
Ford, Ford Madox, 125
Fussell, Edwin, 29
Gallagher, Tess, 92
Ginsburg, Allen, 71
Gray, Richard, 49
Green, Michelle, 31
Greenspan, Ezra, 82
Gunn, Thom, 127
Hannah, Barry, 21
Harrison, Jim, 7
Hassan, Ihab, 10
Hemingway, Ernest, 124-125
Hawthorne, Nathaniel, 76
Hibbard, Allen, 27, 44
Hugo, Richard, 67-81
Hollander, John, 27
Hough, Graham, 44
Joyce, James, 15-16, 58, 126
Kalstone, David, 57
Kaplan, Robert B., 59
Kazin, Alfred, 34
Kerouac, Jack, 6, 70-71,72, 75, 87, 89, 123-124
Kitchen, Judith, 79
Larkin, Philip, 7, 127
Lawrence, D.H., 6, 8, 9-25, 26, 32, 33, 35, 43, 48, 49, 96, 126, 127
Leavis, F.R., 126
Lowell, Robert, 46-67, 68, 75
Lowry, Malcolm, 35
Mallea, Eduardo, 28

Mueller, Jenny, 109-122
Mueller, Lisel, 110
Nabokov, Vladimir, 12-124
Nathanson, Tenney, 46
O'Brien, Tim, 6, 97-108, 125
O'Hara, Frank, 70, 71, 79, 123
Ortega y Gasset, Jose, 22
Otto, Rudolph, 111
Paglia, Camille, 31, 33, 106
Paramenter, Ross, 18
Parini, Jay, 87
Pinkney, Tony, 126
Poe, Edgar Allen, 29, 33, 76, 126
Poirier, Richard, 7, 8
Pounds, Wayne, 29
Pynchon, Thomas, 10
Ramke, Bin, 112
Roethke, Theodore, 78
Rosenberg, Harold, 41
Rothenberg, Jerome, 23
Said, Edward, 43
Schneidau, Herbert, 28
Shetley, Vernon, 60
Smith, Huston, 26
Snyder, Gary, 72-73, 78, 114
Sontag, Susan, 11
Stafford, William, 68-81
Stanton, Elizabeth Cady, 106
Stewart, Lawrence D., 31
Tate, Allen, 127
Twain, Mark, 124
Van Ghent, Dorothy, 71